MISGUIDED

My summer in Greek tourism

Ruard Wallis de Vries

Printed Worldwide
First Printing 2022
First Edition 2022

Published by Ishin-Denshin, London

ISBN: 978-1-3999-0326-4

10 9 8 7 6 5 4 3 2 1

MISGUIDED

for Bente

Contents

Part I

Self-Taught-the-Hard-Way

1. Nothing but a Driver

Silently, Lambros Mangas sipped his Greek coffee, watching the trees behind the runway bend dangerously in the southern wind.

 "You know," he said, "at my age, this stuff isn't so much fun anymore. This is crazy business. Here goes my Saturday for a handful of idiots."

He slowly turned his head in my direction. He looked tired, his eyes a little droopy. "And all this because of you, *my boy*." He reached out and patted me on the back, a little too forcefully for comfort.

Lambros Mangas, the self-taught-the-hard-way managing director of Mangas Travel, shouldn't have been at the Athens airport at all on this windy day in April 1992. The thing was, as the newly appointed tour operator for SolAir Netherlands, he was responsible for all the SolAir Mainland Greece tours that spring. Which is where the trouble started. SolAir was new to the Greek tourism market, and its CEO in Holland had decided that all tours would go ahead no matter what, even if only three or four travelers had booked. Mangas had just hired me to lead the SolAir tours. He had also just discovered that I had lied to him about my driver's license: I didn't have one. So here we were, Mangas and I, at the Athens airport. I would welcome the guests, and – just for today – Mangas would just play the driver for a tour group of just four people.

Earlier that day, Mangas had shown me the cute but small Nissan Cherry Vanette. He was all confidence and grand gestures: "Perfect for you, a driver and four people!" I tried to warn him that the four backseats offered worryingly little legroom for four adult Dutchmen – in fact, Nissan itself advertised two of these seats as for *occasional* use only. To use this dinky toy for a seven-day tour and more than 2,000 kilometers would be a recipe for disaster. But Mangas paid no heed to my words of warning: "Everything will be *super fine*! Just remember one thing: Today I am nothing but a driver."

I began to feel ill at ease as soon as I'd collected the four guests from the arrivals hall. Our group consisted of a petite, moody-looking couple in their sixties, and two men traveling alone. One was tall and skinny, the other short and overweight, but what they had in common was that they were clearly not happy to discover the tour group was so small. Without a word, the members of the group worked themselves into the Cherry Vanette, each facing their own particular physical challenges getting in. I didn't have a chance to worry about that though, because self-taught-the-hard-way, nothing-but-a-driver Mangas was struggling to hoist the four large suitcases onto the roof rack – perilously hanging from one side of the vehicle, his full weight causing the van to lean sideways. I quickly jumped to counterbalance the load, standing in the doorway on the other side to keep the van from tipping over, thus sending new shockwaves through the Vanette. As the group inside fearfully pitched back and forth, Mangas and I made frantic attempts to clamp the tentacles of the bungee cords around the suitcases.

When eventually we secured everything as best as we could, a hush fell over the van. Mangas started the engine, glanced into his rearview and whispered to me in Greek: "Don't forget. Today I am just the driver, nothing else."

As we drove off, I started thinking maybe this would work out after all. But just then, as the van climbed the overpass toward the highway to Athens, a gust of wind hit us. It picked up the little vehicle, and for a moment everyone on board had the impression that the Cherry Vanette (three meters long, one-and-a-half meters wide, and, with all the roof luggage, almost three meters high) would fly away. A gasp went up from the front of the van to the back and back again to the front. Then, as if nothing had happened, Mangas got the wheels safely back on the asphalt.

Welcome to the SolAir Mainland Greece Tour!

How on earth had I, a twenty-four-year-old Dutch university graduate, found myself playing tour guide for travelers on a Greek tour bus, employed by this hard-boiled, take-no-prisoners, self-taught-the-hard-way Lambros Mangas, Managing Director of Mangas Travel?

It had something to do with love, of course. And with the inevitable question anyone in a serious relationship with someone from abroad must face: Where are we going to settle? It was high time for my Greek girlfriend, Vasso, and me to make that decision. We had met in our student days and nothing was more natural for us than to continue together afterwards. She had survived a Dutch winter, and I had survived the summer heat of Athens. Both countries seemed good enough to us, and we had started learning each other's language with enthusiasm. The deal we had come up with was simple and logical: Whoever found a job first would decide where we were going to live. At least, that was what we said to my Dutch family and friends, because by then we had agreed between us that there was, in fact, only one place we wanted to be: Greece.

So, when Vasso landed a teaching job in the old Athenian district of Plaka, I wasted no time boarding a plane to Greece with a couple of suitcases, a BA in international relations, and a heart full of expectation. During my first weeks and months in Athens, I worked hard on my Greek. It wasn't good enough yet to keep a conversation going, but there were days when I felt I was getting there. I was looking for work in Athens, preferably work in line with my degree. After all, I had written my final thesis on the Greek accession to the European Economic Community. OK, I knew I had emigrated to a country where jobs for university graduates were not exactly there for the taking. Then again, I hadn't worried too much about it; I was in love and overjoyed to be in Athens. Plus, I had dragged a very heavy electrical typewriter through customs with a plan to continue writing. And to travel. To travel a lot.

After a month or two without any progress on the job front, I began to realize that maybe I wasn't going to do a lot of traveling, what with Vasso working full-time hours and a bank account that was rapidly approaching zero. My writing didn't go that well either. Soon I was leafing through the *Athens News* on a daily basis, hunting for job vacancies. I wanted a regular job. Nothing more, nothing less. Any job, really. But how to find my way in the Athenian jungle?

I often went jogging on the green hills around the Acropolis. From there, the city looked like an endless tangle of concrete, which seemed to me to accurately reflect the complex structure of Greek society. Athenian friends with piles of diplomas complained about this system, too – apparently it was a matter of knowing the right person in the right place. Enter Mr. Hans Zevenbergen, political attaché at the Dutch Embassy in Athens. In his office, he kindly offered me Douwe Egberts coffee with a Verkade biscuit. Rather pompously, in retrospect, I set my thesis about Greece and the EU on his desk. As he hardly looked at it and did not say altogether much, I decided to ask him directly if it was true that some of the embassy staff were recruited locally. He replied that this only applied to Greek staff who occasionally did translations or secretarial work. Then he started to explain at length something I already knew: If I wanted to try the official selection process for young academics at the Ministry of Foreign Affairs, I would have to do so in the Hague. At the end of our talk, Zevenbergen did hand me an A4 sheet listing the opening hours of a Dutch library and the times of the weekly tea party hosted by the Dutch Embassy women, both at the same address. He seemed a little sorry that he could not do more for me. When we said goodbye, he suggested that I try working in tourism, as a tour guide, for example. "Maybe not a bad move if you want to prepare yourself for our ministry's selection process."

Playing tour guide? A slave to the tourist industry, an instrument in the hands of Greek tour operators and sleazy bus drivers? At the mercy of a bunch of grumpy tourists, who would be bombarding me with the silliest of questions? *Where's the post office, the pharmacy, the toilets?* I quietly laughed it off. Never!

A few days later, on my way to the bank in the hope that I still had some Dutch cash left, a big tour bus blocked my way at Syntagma Square. The doors opened and before I knew it, I was in the middle of a group of elderly Dutch compatriots on holiday. A sharp Dutch voice rose from their midst: "Ladies and gentlemen! This way please! In ten minutes we will be at Taverna Roof Garden!" The owner of the voice, a young woman with resolute blonde hair and a pronounced set of Dutch front teeth, held aloft a colorful umbrella, although it was clear it wasn't going to rain that day. She wore a spotless white blouse, a neat blue skirt that just about covered her knees and a badge that said *Hallo ik ben Irma.*

Yes, Irma was the genuine article, a 100-percent Dutch tour guide – and Irma's job was all the embassy had to recommend. As she and her group headed off toward Plaka, I checked my bank balance. A little over two hundred guilders left. Which meant no Taverna Roof Garden for the foreseeable future, let alone money to go and see this country. In fact, it would only be a matter of days before I'd be totally dependent on Vasso's modest salary.

Playing tour guide? Maybe not a bad move after all.

On our way to the hotel, tightly packed into the Nissan Cherry Vanette, self-taught-the-hard-way Lambros Mangas began to grow into his role as driver. He gave a short tour of the city ("In front you see Acropolis, on your right Zeus Temple.") and handed the suitcases down to the guests as they disembarked, with the friendliest of smiles. But all was not well. While I was busy arranging complimentary welcome drinks, the passengers huddled in a corner of the hotel lounge for an impromptu meeting. Mangas meanwhile had installed himself at the hotel bar, chatting with a group of his business cronies, paying no mind to the four Dutch travelers or me. Before I could even start my itinerary speech, the wife of the moody couple, an Auntie Millie with silver-rimmed glasses and gray hair pulled tightly into a bun, cleared her throat: "Tell me something... Do you intend for us to travel inside that little biscuit box the entire week?"

The question sounded unmistakably like a threat. "Er, yes, I'm afraid so," I had no choice but to answer. The response, then, from Auntie Millie came down to a pronouncement that if that were indeed the case, she would not be moving one step further. She suffered from swollen legs, and the short ride from the airport had already been too much. Her husband nodded in agreement after every sentence, not uttering a word.

Ed and Henk, the two single men, backed her up in unison. They really weren't the most difficult of guys, but it wouldn't do to hunch in that fetal position for a whole day – let alone a week. Maybe I could still arrange for a slightly larger Ford

Transit, they suggested. That didn't seem like a bad idea to me either, so I went to discuss with Mangas, who, of course, was nothing but a driver, but still… In this fashion, I shuttled back and forth between the opposing sides for quite a while, true to the tour guide's dictum of "It's never the customer's fault." I didn't make an inch of progress. In the end, it was Auntie Millie, who struck the winning blow when, at some point in the negotiations she remarked just loudly enough that "that driver isn't a driver at all, if you ask me."

Mangas rose and slowly approached our table. Smiling warmly, he regarded each member of the group. His droopy eyes then sought out the heart of the problem and came to rest on Auntie Millie. At this point, choosing the correct words was vital: "My dear lady," he began. The driver had now definitively risen above his nothing-but-a-driver status. "You must understand" that it was now Saturday afternoon, that the company would never be able to find another van before the start of the journey on Sunday morning, that we were all only human and that if everyone would just try to cooperate a little—. But Auntie Millie did not let him finish: "Yes, yes, you can try, I know you!" *I know your kind*, she had probably wanted to say, "If there isn't a better bus tomorrow, I'll take the first plane back home!"

That one hurt.

No objection came from the other members of the group, and what's more, they stood squarely behind their leader. Mangas realized that the fight had been lost. Defeated, he muttered something like, "I'll see what I can do," and staggered back to the bar. He remained there sulking with his business friends for a while, while I fed the group all the practical information needed for the week's tour.

Mangas soon called me over to the bar. He claimed that his staff had called up half of Athens, but no one had a suitable van available. He would find a solution, he said, but when he tried to slip out of the hotel unnoticed, Auntie Millie made him freeze in his tracks with a loud "Remember what we said!"

The next morning I arrived at the hotel fifteen minutes early. When I saw Mangas already waiting at the hotel entrance, I knew that something was wrong. Without saying a word, he grabbed me by the arm and led me to the main road. There, he introduced me to a balding man in sunglasses, his large belly poking out through a tight-fitting blazer – the archetypal tour driver. This man just had to belong to a large tour bus somewhere. And lo and behold, there it was: a blue-gray Mercedes tour bus, upholstered and air-conditioned, with a toilet in the back and no fewer than fifty-four seats. A furious Mangas tightened his grip on my arm. "Listen. What I said to the driver, I also say to you: I want you to take a picture of that group in front of this bus, so I can send it to the Netherlands." (Two weeks later, these pictures would accompany a long letter to the CEO of SolAir Netherlands. If they were so eager to organize roundtrip excursions at all costs, well then, fine, Mangas was perfectly capable of arranging that. Look at these pictures – the best bus in town! Incidentally, the bill was attached to the photo, because there was no way in hell that Mangas was going to pay for any of that shit.)

Newly reassured as the messenger bearing good news, I entered the hotel lounge. The cloud of tension in which the four guests were waiting immediately lifted when I told them about the bus. They brought their luggage outside and the driver ushered everyone smoothly onto the fifty-four-seater. Mangas had disappeared into thin air. The doors closed with the crisp sound of something that was being hermetically sealed, and we started cruising down Stadiou Avenue. Mangas had been right the previous day: everything would be super fine.

Behind me, I heard Auntie Millie's whisper resonating through the empty bus: "Well, now, this wasn't necessary either."

2. Overqualified

So, how did I go from realizing that my future in Greece would have to be in tourism to being hired by Lambros Mangas, the self-taught-the-hard-way Captain Jack Sparrow of the Athens tourism industry?

After witnessing Irma and her group make their way toward Taverna Roof Garden, I wrote a pile of application letters to all the Dutch tour operators I could think of. At that point I felt it was the only way to get me out of my Hellenic mid-winter slump.

Yes, a slump. A dip, trouble in paradise, call it what you will, but I was in deep. Every Athenian winter day was cold, with a constant drizzle. Whenever the sun showed its face, I'd rush straight out to bask in it, in my new and optimistic summer clothes, and would promptly catch a cold. Internet, email and mobile phones weren't around yet, so communication was slow. This was Athens in the early nineties. The metro and the major public works that would force the city into the twenty-first century were just ideas at this point. Athens was a smelly, messy city generally unfriendly to foreigners, and especially the Dutch. Our foreign minister had recently made some ill-advised comments about EU recognition of the former Yugoslav Republic of Macedonia, more-or-less suggesting the Greeks shouldn't make so much of a fuss about the new country's name. In immediate response, a popular Greek radio station announced a boycott of all Dutch products. It was a resounding success: Gouda, Edam, Heineken and Frisian milk lay on the grocery shelves unsold. The Dutch newspaper *De Telegraaf* was screaming blue murder as the boycott cost the Netherlands millions of guilders per day. And to make things worse, Vasso, too, would get touchy when the subject was raised. In short, I found out the hard way that Greece was more than just a sunny holiday destination. I was beginning to realize it was a country with uncertain borders and potentially inflammable political conflicts. In summer, it was all Mediterranean Sea, sun and smiles, but in winter, Greece showed its less carefree, Balkan side.

All of this strengthened my resolve to look for employment in the tourism industry, for I was no longer so convinced that my future lay in this complicated country. And I wanted to get out of Athens and see the countryside before I missed my chance. The only way to do so without money was, very simply, to find a way to get paid to travel. Enter the tourism sector – perhaps not such a bad move after all.

Writing to Dutch tour operators, I bragged about my language competencies and my "profound knowledge of Greek history and culture," making little effort to disguise my status as a young graduate. I received five letters back, three of which indicated that they would like to check me out when their representatives returned to Athens.

So I waited, leafed through job vacancies, went out jogging, caught a few colds and waited some more. In the meantime, Vasso spotted an English-language advertisement in a Greek newspaper: "Gold Star Travel seeks English-speaker for clerical work." I quickly translated my resume into English and sent it in. Three days later, I got a call from a woman whose name was Lucinda and whose accent sounded very American. "Hello Ruard, we would like you to come by."

I was already on my way.

Approaching the office of Gold Star Travel, I realized how nervous I was. Athens once again seemed unwilling to help me out, and I was going to be late. The trolley was moving in hiccups through an endless traffic jam. I squeezed myself out of the crowded vehicle and hailed a taxi, which ended up not going much faster than the bus through the same traffic. I was going to be very late. Once there, it took forever to find Gold Star Travel listed in the lobby directory. Having finally found the right door, I was just about to ring the bell when I hesitated. What on earth was I doing here? Why didn't I just go back to the Netherlands, register at a job center and apply for unemployment benefits? And then, after a dozen or so job interviews, I'd take my seat somewhere behind a tidy desk in a well-lit office alongside pleasant colleagues. I'd have coffee breaks with *stroopwafel* and lighthearted chats stoking the rivalry between the teams of Feyenoord and Ajax. There would be weekend trips to Paris or London, and holidays to Greece whenever possible. For the first time, it seemed to me like a rather attractive option. But damn it, I shouldn't give up that fast! Was that really what I wanted, to return home after only two lousy months abroad and set up camp in my parents' attic? I had hardly gotten to know Greece yet and was still hungry to experience something new. And if that weren't enough, did I really want to see Vasso only during the holidays? Don't be a wimp, I told myself. Ring that doorbell!

Lucinda was a Greek-American woman of about forty years old, a professional smile set firmly on her face. She showed me around the chic office with some pride: modern black desks, spotless white floors, and Tina Turner's "Simply the Best" ringing out from four tiny black speakers hung from the ceiling. "Well, Ruard," she began. It didn't matter that I was late. "It's Athens, I know how it is," she said in a sympathetic voice. Then she began to describe the job opening as enticingly as possible. "Yeah, you see, it's basically like this…" They were looking for a *boy Friday* to operate the telephone and telex whenever Lucinda was at the airport doing transfers. But if I wanted to, I could do those transfers as well, which mostly entailed accompanying groups of travelers to and from the airport. Her pen traced its way down my resume – she had highlighted half of it already. "Pretty neat that you speak some extra languages. We can give you the basic salary to start. We are a small company, as you know, but believe me, Ruard, there are possibilities to grow professionally." It was a short interview but we said goodbye warmly. I sensed she would call me back for sure. "Goodbye now, Ruard."

On the way home, I got off the trolley a few stops early to walk the last stretch and let everything sink in. Would I really have to play Lucinda's assistant for the entire glorious Greek summer? Over the next few days, I asked around about the basic Greek salary. It turned out to be substantially lower than Dutch unemployment benefits. I banished that thought once more from my mind right then and there. At Lucinda's doorbell I had made my decision: I would stay.

There had been no further responses to my Dutch applications. But before I could take any further action on that front, Lucinda was on the phone again. Did I want to come by to talk to her business partner? Because I happened to be one of their three final candidates.

That was just the ego boost I needed. In a much improved mood, I hopped on a fast trolley to meet Lucinda. With the promise of an early spring in the air, Athens seemed to be on my side again. This time I arrived at Gold Star Travel with time to spare.

Lucinda's business partner was a very pleasant Greek man of about fifty. He gave me some English and German texts to translate back and forth. Ha! Now here was a job I liked! He asked me how serious I was about my intentions to go into tourism. This was not an unexpected question, and I had rehearsed my answer at home. "Mainly, I hope to gain experience this year. Test the waters. And if I like it, I would like to make a career out of it." Lucinda's partner smiled as if he wasn't quite convinced but surged onward explaining how important it was to offer excellence in this business: "Don't forget that our guests have worked for their holidays all year!" He rounded it off with what he said was the golden rule in tourism: "Whatever happens, always keep smiling!"

We said goodbye with a warm handshake.

Not long after, Lucinda called me. "I'm so sorry, Ruard, but we've taken someone else." I was, she said, overqualified. No surprise there, really. Lucinda just needed an assistant, not some restless young academic who would take flight at the first opportunity. It was back to job vacancies and Greek lessons.

Soon another opportunity opened up: The daily English-language *Athens News* was looking for a proofreader, and they interviewed me for the job. While I was waiting on the results, Lucinda called again, out of the blue. "Still looking for a job, Ruard? You can start next week!"

What it came down to was this: If I was crazy enough to accept their terms, we would have a deal. The first month would earn me 70,000 drachmae (around three hundred euros), although the Greek basic salary was 80,000. "It is only February, the season is still young and the income uncertain," she explained. No doubt I could understand that, couldn't I?

I understood. But I didn't call Athens News to cancel a possible proofreader job.

Three days before my career in tourism with Lucinda would begin, the phone rang. It was before 9 a.m., an unusual hour for our phone to ring. Vasso answered and made a strange face. She said in Greek, "Yes, he's here." Then she handed me the phone and whispered that it was some Dutch person, a certain Jan. "Does he speak Greek?" I mimed. "Yes!" she mimed back, "Pretty well!"

What followed was my first conversation with Jan de Brouwer, the Dutch representative of SolAir Netherlands in Greece. He had received my application letter through SolAir headquarters and wanted to meet with me about a job. In fact, he wanted to meet me right away. He was going to move to Crete in a few days' time and SolAir urgently needed someone to handle things in Athens. Could I please come and see him this same afternoon?

There was something funny about the way Jan spoke. It was all very fast, and he sounded stressed. Was that what happened to you after ten years in Greek tourism? He kept firing away: "How long have you known your girlfriend? Any wedding plans? You do realize that you'd pocket more money just by sitting on your ass in Holland, right?"

When I reached the address Jan had given me, it took me a while to find the SolAir sign, which turned out to be no more than a small sticker pasted next to a huge sign for Mangas Travel. Upon closer inspection, I saw that part of the SolAir sticker had been blocked out with a strip of white tape, but you could still read the text behind it: *We know Turkey like no other.*

I walked up the stairs and into the office of SolAir/Mangas Travel, remarkably more confident than I'd been at Lucinda's door. She was now my plan B, and moreover, I would get to talk to a fellow countryman who was apparently in true need of me. And goodness, was he in need of me! Jan almost pushed me into his office, sat me in a chair and started talking immediately. He was a pale, skinny guy in his mid-thirties, his Dutch staccato punctuated with Greek curses. "Yes, I am moving to Crete on Tuesday, *gamòto*! That's where most of the work is, you see. Not in Athens. But there's been no news from the mothership – nothing. Until I got this from them." He pulled out my crumpled letter, the one I'd sent to SolAir Netherlands weeks earlier. Scrutinizing my resume, he remarked irritably: "I also took Ancient Greek at school, just so you know."

He put my letter away and continued: "From April onwards, there are tours. You're going to lead those. Pays well. Mykonos, Santorini, Crete, Peloponnese, Delphi, all the way up to Meteora. You have to read up on all of that. Here, read this.

Baedeker's Greece. The Bible. Everything you need to know is in there. In between tours, you will do transfers. Up and down from the airport to the hotels. Glyfada, Lagonisi, Nea Makri. Good money. Too bad Lambros isn't here. Mr. Mangas. You know what? Come back tomorrow, I'll introduce you to him then. And I'll talk you through the tours. Mainland and the islands. Can you handle a telex? That *malakismèno* device doesn't work half the time. How fast do you type?"

Late that evening, I got home exhausted but excited. I knew I was going to do some traveling soon.

3. Keep on Smiling

The day that followed my first meeting with Jan at Mangas Travel was a rainy one. In fact, on the way to the office it started to rain so violently that I had to duck into a shop to buy my first Greek umbrella. As I arrived at the office, I shook the umbrella out and opened it back up to let it dry. Almost as one, the entire staff of Mangas Travel jumped up from their desks, frantically waving and gesturing for me to close the umbrella up immediately. "Bad luck! It brings bad luck!" they cried.

Fellow Dutchman Jan ignored the racket and jumped right ahead into his one-day bluff-your-way-into-tourism course. "*Sto diavolo*! When will that telex arrive? You should be able to do that by tonight, sending telexes. But that *bastardismèno* machine isn't working again. Have you written down the send formula? Yes? Are you sure?"

That day, he crammed me with all the knowledge he'd gained in his ten years as tour guide, never skipping a beat. How high do you hold a sign up at the airport arrivals hall? (At shoulder height, never at crotch height.) How do you hand over the room keys to guests on arrival at the hotel? (Discreetly, so the group members won't see each other's room numbers.) How do you divide the tips between yourself and the driver? (Fifty-fifty, always.) There were lists and lists of telephone numbers – for local guides, C-class hotels, B-class hotels, hospitals and, of course, the little roadside cafe that served the best yogurt with honey and walnuts in all of the Peloponnese.

In the middle of all this, while Jan and I were focusing intently on the telex screen, I heard a stir behind me. A hefty, bearded man was performing circus tricks with Chaplin-like dexterity for the amusement of the office workers. As I turned, I saw him balancing my brand-new umbrella on his shoe. Overloaded as I was with the morning's onslaught of information, I was not in the mood for jokes and started in with a "Sorry, could you—" but Jan hushed me mid-sentence. "Don't worry," he offered quietly, "he always gives everything back."

Who was that dancing imbecile, now busy in the act of balancing my umbrella on his awesome Greek nose? No one in the office seemed disturbed by his antics, even as he flirted with bad luck by opening the umbrella indoors. He stepped into a spacious office and took a seat behind a large oak desk, waving my umbrella above his head. Could this man be...? He shouted "ELENI!" and a girl stood and walked over to him. Yes, this dancing imbecile was none other than the managing director of Mangas Travel, the man himself. Jan explained in a conspiratorial tone that the atmosphere here was fine, really, and that Mangas was basically a nice guy. And by the way, did I have a driver's license? When I told him I didn't, Jan let out another series of curses. Could I get one ASAP, please, because in four or five weeks the first tour groups would arrive.

"JAN!" came a roar from behind the big oak desk. "ONE SEC!" Jan shouted back, nearly as loud. Then he asked quickly if I had thought about a salary. I asked him how much he earned, which turned out to be the equivalent of six hundred euros per month – a very decent amount at the time. Moreover, he said, you could earn an additional twenty a day as a bonus while on tour. Just before we entered Mangas' office, Jan whispered, "Keep your mouth shut about that goddamn driver's license!"

His name was Lambros Mangas, director of the firm that bore his name. "Self-taught the hard way," as he boasted in his English-language brochures. A large, unkempt bear of a man, an authentic Greek colossus. His motto was written on a bright yellow placard that hung behind his large desk, in plain view of every trembling employee: *New Management Directive: No Work? Fired!*

He took a long look at me, sizing me up. With a sugary sweet smile, he asked Jan in Greek "if this kid was any good." Jan explained hurriedly that I seemed to be the right man for the job and that I also understood Greek pretty well. "Right," Mangas continued, entirely unperturbed. He leaned over to me and asked in Greek, "Do you have a driver's license? Do you love your wife? Are you planning to stay in Greece? Do you always have an umbrella with you?" When I managed to answer back in Greek to the barrage of questions without stuttering (including that lie about the driver's license), Mangas leaned back in his leather chair with a contented air about him. He then launched into a monologue in English about how dispensable, replaceable and multi-employable every single one of his staff members were. Flexibility was crucial, he repeated, because tourism was as volatile as—, here Mangas' giant right hand motioned up and down, as if he were playing with a yo-yo. He asked if I'd been in the army. No? Too bad, otherwise I'd know exactly what to compare tourism to. One year you're swimming in dough while the next you might be shoveling shit. He asked me what salary I anticipated. A few thoughts ran quickly through my mind: Would he know that I had very little choice? It was either Lucinda or Lambros

Mangas at this point. I couldn't afford to make any mistakes here, so, of course, I made one instantly. I replied that I wanted to earn more than the minimum wage. "That's settled then," Mangas said, "The minimum wage plus the daily allowances. Right?" And with that, he offered me my umbrella back. When I got up to take it, he pulled it away again and said, "Rule number one: Keep on smiling. Always keep smiling. And from now on, always watch out for your umbrella. A tour guide cannot do without one. Right?"

"Right!" I smiled. Only then did I get my umbrella back.

The first task in my brand-new job was to call Lucinda and inform her I had just found other employment. She was silent for a few seconds and then let out an exasperated "Oh my Goddd!" But soon enough she said she understood.

Next, self-taught-the-hard-way Mangas came to tell me the news in person: There was no work, at least not until the first tour group showed up in April. I could have figured that much out myself. It was only February, and until April there were hardly any bookings for the hotels around Athens. Mangas saw my disappointment and decided to soften his stance somewhat. He renamed the period up to April my *internship*. I could go wherever I wanted, ask him and his staff all I wished, and gather as much wisdom from Mangas himself as I desired. As the cherry on top, he offered me a trip, "along with your *wife*, if she wants": a three-day excursion to the Peloponnese, a trip reserved exclusively for his Greek clientele. At the end of my internship (which, indeed, culminated in a dreary three-day trip to the Peloponnese amid a troupe of elderly Greeks), there were still hardly any bookings for the SolAir roundtrips. Mangas asked me to sit and grab a pen, and started pacing his office. Suddenly, his voice came thundering down, dictating a one-and-a-half-page telex to SolAir Netherlands, a baroque story spooling out in all directions, peppered with words like "unrealistic," "unprofitable" and "superfluous." In other words: *No work? Fired!*

The telex also stated that it would not be economical to organize tours for the handful of tourists who had booked up to that point. That was why Lambros Mangas himself was personally informing the SolAir head office of his decision to cancel all upcoming roundtrips for that spring. It was rather a shame that the first telex I'd send from this office would also be my letter of termination – but a termination from what, exactly? I still hadn't worked a single day.

4. The Voucher

Mykonos, a beautiful spring evening in late April.

In the company of Toon and Nellie, a pleasant forty-something couple from Eindhoven, I was enjoying the sunset on the terrace of a picturesque seaside taverna. Toon had secretly booked this trip for their fifteenth wedding anniversary, and together the two of them formed the entirety of the first ever SolAir Greek Islands Tour. There were no complaints from their side about the size of the group – they didn't need other people to enjoy themselves. Once we'd arrived on Mykonos, they told me that I could have a little holiday to myself if I wanted, too. Lucky me! The sun was shining, and the island was in full bloom.

As the man in charge, I was in possession of the trip vouchers. Vouchers are like a secret set of keys to the world: They open doors that remain closed to ordinary mortals. With a voucher, a tour guide can board airplanes and ferries at no cost and dine at restaurants without paying a bill. Just a simple wave of a voucher and you can bypass the lengthy hotel check-in process. Here in Mykonos, with the effortless display of my voucher at the reception desk, our room keys were promptly offered up.

On the first night with my so-called group, seated outside at a seaside taverna, I showed Toon and Nellie the meal voucher and told them to order anything they'd like. They turned with appreciative eyes toward the large aquarium next to our table where a few fearsome lobsters were vying for a bit of breathing room. "Well, dear, what do you think?" Nellie whispered. That was the cue for the friendly, mustachioed waiter to step forward and introduce us to the impressive malacostracans. "Are you sure it's ok?" Toon asked me. "Sure!" I replied with a smile. After all, I was in the possession of a dinner voucher.

We ordered lobster for three.

Either the big boss of SolAir in the Netherlands wanted to do me a huge personal favor, or he had completely lost his marbles, because he decided to green light every roundtrip for which at least two people had booked. That's how self-taught-the-hard-way Lambros Mangas found himself back on the phone with me, a mere two weeks after the sending of that bombastic telex of early termination. In his sweetest voice, he asked if I had found another job. Indeed, I had. I'd just started work as a proofreader for *Athens News*, but Mangas didn't need to know that. When I met him the next day, I found him behind his desk, sullen and resigned, complaining what a waste of time and money it would be to have to arrange all those hotels and airport transfers for groups of only two. And my job? His voice rose again to its thunderous volume as he slapped tickets and vouchers down on his large oak desk: "Saturday, you fly to Mykonos. Monday, you fly to Santorini… Wednesday, you take the boat to Crete…"

I realized my proofreading days had come to an end.

Lying in bed that night, Jan's crash course in tourism came to mind again: "Tell lots of stories on the bus. You don't have to read them the complete Greek mythology but do churn out plenty of juicy stories. The Hercules stuff when you come through the Argolis. The entire Trojan War whenever you think the group is up for it. And when you're riding through some ugly town like Patras or Corinth, bring up all the nymphs, muses, graces and courtesans Zeus slept with. Keep them occupied, keep them amused. Info cocktails, welcome drinks, transfers, check-ins, check-outs… Stay friendly no matter what, but never, ever be their doormat. If you don't know what to answer, make something up. You are the tour guide, you know everything. If you tell them in the morning that Cretans eat *moussaká* with their hands, you can be sure that half the group will try it that evening. And whatever happens, make sure you never lose your vouchers."

Within a few minutes of ordering the lobsters, a slight sense of unease entered my mind as I reminded myself that this island tour was going to cost SolAir a lot of money. I slipped into the restaurant and asked to see the voucher again – "I need to check something," I told the mustachioed waiter. He handed the voucher back to me, with a suspicious look. Right away I saw the text I had not bothered to take note of earlier: *Tourist menu only*. But it was too late. The lobsters had already gone into a large pot of boiling water. The waiter became rather formal with me now. The order was already in, so lobster it would be. The difference in the price covered by the vouchers came out to ten thousand drachmae: Exactly the amount that I had earned in my first two days as a tour guide.

It was my turn now to be disappointed. Luckily the tourist menu included unlimited wine and, it must be said, the lobsters were absolutely delicious. Gradually, my mood improved. The "No lobster with a voucher" story came out by the end of our second bottle of retsina. Toon immediately offered to pay the difference – actually, he insisted. Perhaps I surrendered my resistance a little too quickly, and with that my being a tour guide. I decided to tell the happy couple how it had come about that I first did, then didn't, then did again, then didn't again but finally did get hired for the SolAir roundtrip tours in Greece. The wine kept flowing, and Toon and Nellie let out one roar of laughter after the other.

After a week of sun, sea and voucher fun, I found myself back at the airport with Toon and Nellie. As we hugged goodbye, Toon palmed me an envelope. As soon as he and Nellie passed the security check, I opened it. I noticed the money first, then the paper it was wrapped in. In elegant handwriting it read, "ONLY valid for two lobsters."

5. Undercover Guiding

Remember the group of four led by the fearsome Auntie Millie, who had left self-taught-the-hard-way Lambros Mangas no choice but to rent an air-conditioned fifty-four-seater Mercedes tour bus, while he was pretending, unsuccessfully, to be nothing but a driver?

We return to this special group on the day the tour bus departs Athens to begin its SolAir Mainland Greece Tour...

Guiding at Greek tourist sites is not a job open to just anyone. Archaeological sites and monasteries are the exclusive domain of officially licensed guides. And who are these officially licensed guides? According to Greek law, they are the happy few who successfully graduate from the one-and-only Greek Tour Guide School. So, when you see a figure guiding a group of tourists at famous sites like Mycenae, Delphi, Ancient Olympia or the Acropolis, you can be sure that he or she is a tried and tested graduate of that singular institution.

For any foreign tour guide, Greek archaeological sites are strictly no-go areas when it comes to guiding, therefore. But that wasn't going to be the case for our Auntie Millie Tour. After the episode with the Mercedes fifty-four-seater, Lambros Mangas made it his aim to cut back as many unnecessary expenses as possible. That's why he decided, ultimately, to cancel the hiring of licensed guides, even though we planned to visit quite a number of sites where they were mandatory.

"You want to try real guiding?" Mangas had asked me back in Athens, with his most syrupy smile. He knew very well that I had spent the previous two months reading up on every collection of ancient stones in Greece and that I was more than eager to share that knowledge. Indeed, I didn't say no right away, even though several friends had written to me about a Belgian tour guide who had landed in a Greek prison simply because he had pointed a little too obviously at the Acropolis.

Mangas knew the story. "You need to think smart. And that Belgian guy wasn't thinking smart." So, what was he advising me to do, exactly? "Undercover tour guiding," he said. "Keep your hands down, no pointing. No circle of people around you, either – not even a semi-circle!" But what about the Greek law that places a prison sentence on illegal guide work? "Come on now!" Mangas snapped impatiently. "What kind of trouble do you expect from those four? If the cops come after you, just say that you're on a family outing!"

When my small group entered the site of Ancient Corinth, I was completely disoriented for a moment. Then a number of landmarks settled into view. The Doric temple, for instance –

bigger than I'd expected, but oh well, Doric is Doric. The baths had to be diagonally opposite – probably that row of lower-level alcoves there – which meant that we were now standing at the agora. I hastily checked the tiny map I'd brought along, because there was one thing I had not dared tell Mangas: I had never been to Ancient Corinth before.

So, I led the group as discreetly as possible. As I relayed information about the site, kept my sentences short and tried to avoid any subject that might prompt the group to ask more questions. Although I did not detect any guards around, I was careful never to indicate in the direction of any of the antiquities. The group followed along meekly and silently, my undercover guiding effectively thwarting any extra inquiries. That is, until Auntie Millie abruptly pointed at a white building in the distance. "Over there, is that the museum?"

My stress level shot up. Why did she have to talk so loud? Why did she have to *point*?

The building looked like a museum indeed, but not a museum that was in any of my guidebooks. This could mean trouble. I pretended that I had not heard her, and continued along with my undercover tour, making sure I was never at the head of the group. But there was Aunt Millie again, index finger outstretched toward the white building, her voice rising with every word. "Hello? Did you go dea-heaf? The museum!"

We soon began to draw unwanted attention, particularly from a cluster of Greeks wearing badges and loitering near the museum entrance. Were they official guides? It sure looked like they were. It would only be a matter of seconds before they called the guards. Time to lead my group swiftly past for a quick visit to the museum. Now I was in a quandary – I knew nothing about this place. I was going to have to fake it. Let's see, the building had the standard U-shaped museum design. On the left, the usual pottery. We could skip most of that; Auntie Millie had pots and pans at home, anyway. Instead, I moved along to a section of marble carvings on gravestones – that was all recognizable enough to my group. From the looks of it, most were unremarkable Roman copies. Alongside these, however, were some pieces of marble statuary, the remains of female nudes. This was fortuitous because it gave me the opportunity to tell the story of Corinth as the center of prostitution in Ancient Greece – to the point where local prostitutes had the inscription "Follow me" carved in mirror image on the soles of their shoes, thus leaving behind an impression in the sand and dust, luring potential customers their way. That little story drew a laugh from the boys in the group, a perfect moment for me to wrap up the tour. Thank god, the ordeal was over, and now I deserved a large, cold beer. But before I could usher my group safely to the exit, Aunt Millie piped up again. "Excuse me, where can I freshen myself up?"

"Freshen up?" I echoed.

"Yes, the toilet. Where is the toilet?"

I really had no idea.

"I'll find out," she said. "I will ask one of the *real* guides over there."

The guide she addressed was a stern-looking lady in her fifties, who then came over to me.

"So, who do you work for?" she asked in Greek.

"I'm not working. These are my friends!"

"No need to beat around the bush. Are you the Mangas group?"

I was speechless. How did she know?

She put a hand on my shoulder: "Believe me, *my boy*, we all know about your so-called group and your big tour bus. Half of Greece is having a good laugh about it at the moment. And besides, we know your boss a little. Give him our dearest, sweetest, and most *fucking* regards."

And with that, she let me go.

6. Everything Is Business

On the last day of the Auntie Millie Tour, the driver of the fifty-four-seater Mercedes bus, Lazaros, takes center stage. Self-taught-the-hard-way Mangas had asked him to snap a picture of the four guests in front of the tour bus – a photo he planned to send to the CEO of SolAir Netherlands, accompanied by a hefty bill for the rental of the tour bus...

On our drive back to Athens, Lazaros unexpectedly pulled the bus over to the side of the road, parked it and stood up. Then he turned to Aunt Millie and her three companions and announced in flawless English: "I will take a photo of you all!"

The group of four looked at each other in disbelief. "Did we hear that right? Does Lazaros really want to take a photo of us? That moody old fart of a driver who has never uttered one single word this whole time? Look at him now, with his camera in hand. Is that actually a smile on his face? This... this metamorphosis is nothing short of a miracle!"

When I had introduced Lazaros to the group on our first day, Aunt Millie had exclaimed, "Lazaros?! Oh great, our driver is *lazerus!*" meaning "stone drunk" in Dutch. The group chuckled about it for the rest of the tour. Left out of the joke, Lazaros pressed me for a translation. Finally giving in, I explained why they found his name so amusing. He let out a few elaborate curses, comparing Aunt Millie to a she-goat with devil's horns and worse. From that moment on, whenever he was in the group's company, which was mainly at meals, he confined his contributions to sighing and belching, expertly ruining every dinner on the tour.

During my one-day crash course, Jan had told me that tour guides shouldn't join the group for any meals or coffee breaks. Instead, I was supposed to eat with the driver, preferably at a small table discreetly tucked away at the back of the taverna. But Aunt Millie had other plans and invited Lazaros and me over to the group's table during our very first meal, setting an unfortunate precedent for our future dining arrangements. Perhaps she felt some pangs of regret for the hullabaloo over the van, or perhaps it was sympathy for Lazaros and me – we were only doing our jobs, after all. It might have also been that she thought our presence could spark some kind of interesting conversation. Not so: just the opposite, in fact. Lazaros sat through every meal in stony silence. To make matters worse, he somehow always ended up at the head of the table, where the weight of his presence was even more prominently felt. Once finished with his meal, he'd sit there sighing and belching, effectively killing any conversation that might have transpired. The four travelers ate every meal in silence thereafter, excusing themselves from the meal as soon as decency would allow.

After the second of these dining ordeals, Lazaros looked at me and said, "You need a drink. Come with me." He took me to a venue that was the exclusive domain of Greek tour bus drivers: an anonymous roadside cafeteria. Mercilessly lit by a row of fluorescent tubes and filled with tired old furniture and cigarette smoke, the place looked like a waiting room for the nearly departed. Which, in a way, it was. Lazaros' colleagues were all potbellied men, who sat there with beaded *kombolói* in their hands, endlessly lamenting their fates in life. I was soon to discover that Greece was full of such places, as Lazaros would repeat the same routine every evening, with me in tow. Most time in these places was spent staring wistfully at the sixty-year-old "girl" behind the counter, making occasional commentary about what misery Christ and all the saints had poured out upon the world, especially upon the Guild of Greek Tour Bus Drivers. Over the course of such evenings, Lazaros taught me the ins and outs of life on the road and how to go after packs of cigarettes. Cigarettes? "Look," Lazaros explained, "it's simple. Everything is business. Should you ever come here with a full bus, take them to Olympia by Night. The big restaurant. You sit down with the driver at a table near the cash register. Just before you leave, ask the boss for a pack of cigarettes. If all goes well, it contains 10 percent of the total bill, which you share with the driver."

It was becoming increasingly clear to me that the tour bus drivers had a big hand in the tourist business, even if they were just drivers. Say the packs of cigarettes were disappointing at Taverna X and that it happened a few times in a row, the drivers would soon tip each other off about this. Result: The owner of Taverna X might as well close down his business. Tour guides play only a marginal role in this game – they come and go with every new season, but the drivers remain in place. Whether they like it or not, the tour bus driver and the tour guide are thrust together as allies on the hunt for cigarettes. Tour guides who dare opt for restaurants that are not on the drivers' cigarette list in favor of those that are more picturesque will quickly regret it. By now I understood very well to what extent a disgruntled driver could single-handedly destroy an entire trip.

On this last day of the tour, amid the stench and noise of the Athens–Thessaloniki highway, my group and I posed readily for Lazaros, smiling in the sunlight in front of the fifty-four-seater bus. In their enthusiasm, each of the four guests proceeded to take a picture of their traveling companions. How relieved they were that their driver had finally shed his grumpy exterior! Six days of pent-up tension and untapped holiday mood finally found its way out. For the remaining few hours of the trip, there was lots of talk, shoulder-patting and laughter between the driver and the group. Auntie Millie asked Lazaros if he did that on every trip, take pictures of his groups. He smiled a contented smile and said, "Only the special ones."

When I said goodbye to Lazaros, he said that it had been a good tour. "I even started to like them at the end."

"So, are you going to give Mangas those pictures now?"

Lazaros sighed, the way only he could sigh, and looked at me with a mixture of pity and fatigue. "Give him the pictures? Why should I *give* him the pictures? Have you learned nothing at all?"

I got the point. Of course: *Everything* is business.

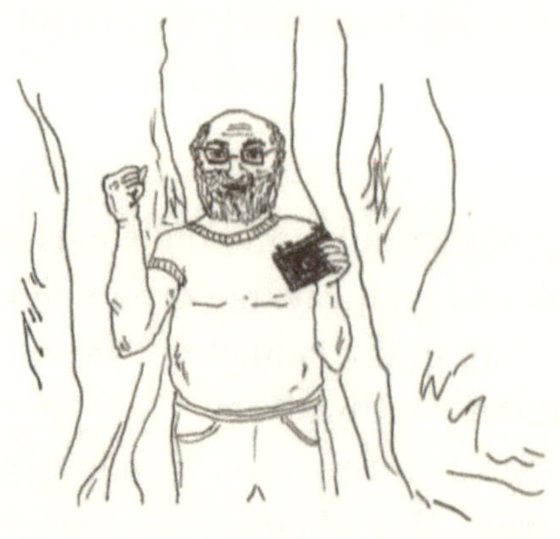

7. Knowledge of Humans

"The ship is about to sail. All visitors are requested to leave the vessel."

A funny announcement, in a way. After all, no one would choose to stay on this ferry longer than necessary. A famous song lyric ran through my head: *We are all just visitors here, of our own device.* Or was it *prisoners?* I sure felt like one, in the current setting of another SolAir Island Tour.

It was early June, and the huge express ferry between Crete and Athens was ready for departure from the port of Heraklion. I was returning to Athens that night, but the man I had been talking to was one of those visitors to whom the announcement had been directed. His name was Vangelis, a soft-spoken, well-mannered tour guide of about thirty. Good-looking in a Cretan way but without all the car honking and shooting of traffic signs so popular with his fellow islanders.

Vangelis had been the tour guide on the bus for the Cretan leg of this island tour. Three days of driving around with a tour group consisting of just two guests had left its marks on him. And not only on him: The first thing I planned to do once back in Athens was to go up to Mangas and hand him my resignation.

And the two guests of the tour? Well, that was another story.

On the ferry, Vangelis urgently needed to know a few things. He bought me a cold beer and found two free chairs on the upper deck. "So," he said, "Tell me what went wrong with this tour."

I looked at him wearily and said, "Everything."

His eyes narrowed. "Start from the beginning."

On the first day of the tour, I found myself nervously waiting in the lobby of the Hotel Stanley in central Athens. I was there to pick up the only two guests who had registered for the Mykonons–Santorini–Crete Island Tour, Mr. Provoost and Ms. Siene. What made me nervous was the message I was about to deliver: They were to move from their four-star to a two-star hotel, from the luxurious Hotel Stanley where they had spent the first week of their vacation to the scruffy Hotel Candia. There was nothing I could do about it. They were now in the hands of Lambros Mangas and his SolAir way of things, which meant: economize wherever possible.

Mr. Provoost and Mrs. Siene turned out to be an older couple whose very presence radiated wealth. Both looked well-preserved for their seventy-odd years. I greeted them with the appropriate respect, and they smiled at my being a fresh graduate giving it a try in Greek tourism. All the same, the message that they were being downgraded to a two-star hotel didn't go well. "Say, can't you arrange for us to remain at the Stanley for these last two nights?" Mr. Provoost demanded, in a rather authoritarian tone.

I told them I couldn't, making sure that they knew it wasn't I who'd come up with this arrangement. Then I ducked out to hail a taxi – never an easy task in central Athens. When one actually pulled up, there was already a passenger inside, leaving room for only two more people. The driver lifted their luggage into the trunk, and Provoost and Siene settled into their seats in the back. What remained outside the taxi was one leftover suitcase and a tour guide. I said I'd meet them at the hotel with their bag, and then made the mistake of carrying it to the Hotel Candia myself. Granted, it was just a short walk, but Athens was hot and oppressive that day and the damn thing didn't have rollers. *Don't be a doormat*, Jan's warning hummed in my head. Too late. From then on, Mrs. Siene never let an opportunity pass to have me carry her luggage.

Once the couple had freshened up a bit at their hotel, they came down to meet me in the lounge of the Candia for the welcome drink that would kick off their SolAir Island Tour. I fished two envelopes out of my bag, one for each. "Mr. Provoost and Ms. Siene, is that right?" I asked.

"No, no," she said tersely. "That is *not* right. My name is Si-èèè-ne. Don't you see the *accent grave* on the first e?"

The situation did not improve when the welcome drink

devolved into a rambling lecture from Provoost on Greek coinage over the centuries. That's where I made my next mistake: Out of a sense of politeness, I'd ask a vaguely interested question, which would only set him off on a much-longer-than-anticipated explanation. Time droned on, but I couldn't find a gracious way to call it a day. Much later than I'd planned, I finally returned to the office to collect the vouchers for the trip. With his arms stretched wide and a look of incomprehension on his face, Mangas said, "A group of two and you spent two hours on the welcome drink? What did you do, *massage* them?"

The next day, we set off on a sightseeing tour of Athens in a large taxi – a Mercedes sedan of the most comfortable kind. But Siène was not in the mood to be pleased by anything that day. The leather seats were sticky. Athens was too busy. The weather was too hot and the Acropolis too much of a climb. I tried to sidestep her complaints, but I had my hands full trying to keep Provoost in check. He seemed determined to show off to Siène his full knowledge of all things Greek and acted as if he himself were the tour guide. If he spotted so much as a stump of a marble column, he would take off toward it before anyone could stop him.

At this point in my story, Vangelis let out a grunt. "Ha! Provoost probably realized that his lady friend was unhappy, and was hell bent on trying to fix it. Apparently by taking charge of the tour."

"You're right," I nodded. "I could see him thinking: *This tour leader is as green as grass. At least I'm here to give some direction to this whole thing.* Except that, to him, giving some direction to the tour meant talking nonstop about everything he knew."

"Ok. Continue, please," Vangelis hurried me to continue.

On our second day, in a seaside restaurant on Mykonos, Provoost spent the entire meal regaling us with stories from his days working for a record company – his meeting with Ray Charles and his nights on the town with Neil Diamond, Neil Sedaka, and God-Knows-Which-Other Neil. Yes, Provoost sure knew how to keep the good times rolling. Meanwhile, Siène herself had nothing but complaints. For starters, their tour leader was some kind of student (a mere boy!) who couldn't even put his shirt on correctly (but her deft adjustments to my collar fixed that!). Then there was the plain fact that no one else was booked for the tour, so no company to add to their twosome to make the experience more interesting. There was also the endless lugging of suitcases... uphill, downhill. She lamented with a loud sigh that she would end up with her back broken because of this, even though I was the one doing all the carrying. And, of course, she was disappointed that we had to fly to Mykonos when a boat trip would have been so much more enjoyable, though this didn't stop her from asking, two days later, why we hadn't booked a nice quick domestic flight to Santorini instead of losing half the day on a slow ferry. But the worst for her were the little plastic jars of honey at breakfast – goodness, they were so difficult to open!

"Wait a second," Vangelis interrupted again. "Wasn't there something about a bed on Santorini as well?"

"Ah yes. Total disaster." When we got to Santorini, the seaside hotel turned out not to be on the seaside but almost fifty meters away from the beach. And when Siène found out that their room had just one double bed, she flipped – from the outset she had been crystal clear about wanting separate beds only. She stormed back to the reception in a rage. The girl at the reception didn't speak a word of English and broke down in tears. It turned out she had mixed up the keys and had given me the room with the two single beds.

Nothing was going to go right on this trip. And as if to prove that point, I then had to relay the news that tomorrow there would only be the overnight boat to Crete, so they would be without a hotel room for a whole day...

"How did *you* take all this?" Vangelis asked me.

"Me?" By the time we made it to the Santorini winery to sample some of that syrupy plonk they tried to pass off as wine, I felt something was going to give soon. I was seated next to Michalis, our local guide for the day, with Provoost and Siène seated awkwardly opposite us, at a table where we had to drink 5 different samples from the same plastic cup. I had bought a bag of pistachios and passed them around, then placed the bag in the middle of the table. Siène, however, picked up the bag and, without pause, began to wolf them down. As the rest of us sat in silence, she ate her way through the entire bag, throwing the shells into an ashtray. Then she stood from the table, walked over to the counter and bought a bottle. Provoost got up as well and began pacing the area. Michalis, watching all this too, whispered, "Get me out of here, they are worse than my parents!"

Provoost and Siène took the news about the overnight ferry very badly. Provoost argued for a plane to Crete instead, and Siène just wanted to go home. In return, I promised that they could keep their room for an extra half day until the time we'd have to leave for the boat, and that calmed them a little. The idea that the hotel would expect payment for that extra room time had not occurred to me. And, of course, the hotel expected just that. The only solution was to call Mangas on his private number. Before I dialed, I rehearsed my angry declaration that would offer him a choice: Either comply, or I'd resign. I would not take no for an answer! But he conceded: "Of course, of course," he sighed, from faraway Athens.

In addition, Mangas had originally told me that our so-called "group" of two would be joining another of his tours in Crete for the last few days. Not so. Now he informed me that there wasn't any such group after all – which meant *another* difficult conversation for me ahead. And believe me, it was, eliciting plenty of heaving and sighing in response. Next, there was the ferry, or rather the lack thereof. The departure time was scheduled for midnight. We arrived by taxi to the harbor at a quarter to twelve, but by half past, there was still no sign of the boat. I offered a round of wine in an attempt to break the awkward silence (even Provoost's formidable stream of grandiose stories had run dry at this point; maybe he'd realized that he had fallen into repetition some time ago). It didn't help. Instead, the wine got Siène going, "How is it possible that this trip is so much more expensive than last year's?" Then she launched into the details of their trip: All the nice hotels in Andalusia, the good service, those professional guides...

I let her vent, and discreetly double checked our boat tickets: B-class, good for three beds, men and women separate, just as the agent had so neatly arranged for me. When the boat finally arrived two hours late, we were all beyond tired. I showed our tickets to the purser, and a member of the crew led us to a cabin: a single cabin, with four beds. "Three persons, one cabin! Please!" he announced, motioning for us to enter.

"Sorry," I said, grinding my teeth, "This ticket is for separate cabins. We don't all want to share one room." I asked Provoost and Siène to wait and went to find the main purser at reception. When he saw me coming, he turned and pretended to be busy with other things. He made me wait. On purpose. I couldn't hold it in anymore. In my best Greek, I let loose a torrent of anger, concluding with, "Look at the ticket, you moron! Is this for one cabin?"

Suddenly, he had time for me. He looked at the ticket and said: "This is B-class, four persons, one cabin."

I exploded. I don't really remember what I said or in what language. At one point, the purser, too, got up and started shouting back. In the end, a quiet guy with an important-looking uniform intervened, and we finally did get our two double cabins. One for the lady and one for the two gents. But that wasn't entirely to Siène's liking either: She didn't want to sleep in a cabin alone. So for the remainder of that night, roughly between 3 and 6 a.m., I had a two-person cabin to myself.

"So, that explains it," Vangelis said.

"That explains what?"

"Let me tell you what happened on my side. When I saw the three of you arrive here on Crete, I saw three wrecks coming off the boat. What I usually do to break the ice is focus on the lady. If the lady is happy, so is the gentleman. So, I got my chance when Provoost and you trekked the Samaria Gorge. First, I took Provoost aside and advised him against the trek, but he insisted he was fit enough to do it. I tried to level with him: *Sir. Believe me. It is a difficult trek, and you are not so young anymore.* That only boosted his fighting spirit. And then I realized it would be a good thing after all if he'd go off to hike the gorge. It would give me a chance to talk to *her*."

"Why talk to her?" I asked. "I don't know what's worse: Talking to Siène for an entire day or trailing behind Provoost through the length of that gorge. The worst was seeing him raise his fist in triumph when we finally made it!"

For the first time, I saw Vangelis smile. "You're the only person I've met who's hated walking the Samaria Gorge. I took Siène to a taverna with a great view. You can see half the gorge from there. It makes people feel small, it makes people talk. And talk she did, believe me. In fact, she poured her heart out to me."

Now I felt a little apprehensive. "Did she tell you how miserable it all was?" I asked.

Again, Vangelis smiled. "Stop worrying, my friend. None of it was about Mangas or any of his small-time crookery. Nor was it about you. In fact, Siène knows you did your damned best to try and fix all the messes. No, it was all about *him*."

I wasn't entirely sure what Vangelis was getting at.

"About Provoost, of course! About him playing the hero. She couldn't stand it anymore! From the moment he took charge of things, she saw what a mistake it had been to go on a trip with him, to *be* with him. They have been fighting every night since. What you saw was just the tip of the iceberg. And if any of it was directed at you, don't take it personally. You were a pawn in their game to defuse some of the tension, like a kid in a bad marriage."

I still wasn't convinced.

"Believe me," Vangelis insisted. "Everything Siène said or did was directed at Provoost."

"But... Surely Mangas made a mess of organizing the whole tour. That couldn't have helped matters."

"Well, in some ways maybe it has. Think about that."

"Last call for visitors! The ship is about to sail. All visitors are requested to leave the vessel immediately!"

As I waved goodbye to Vangelis, I realized that the ordeal was not yet over for Siène and Provoost: They had a few more days booked at a Cretan beach hotel. When I had said goodbye to them earlier that day, Provoost had palmed me a meager tip, saying, "Here you are. You are the only one who made any bit of effort."

I climbed up to the highest deck, ordered another beer and watched the Cretan coastline recede. As I made my way to my bunk in a shared cabin for the night – B-Class, four persons, four beds – I was reminded of a Dutch proverb my grandma liked to say: "Knowledge of humans comes with age."

8. No Work? Fired!

Back in Athens after the overnight boat from Crete, I went straight to Lambros Mangas to tell him I was resigning. Walking up the stairs to his office, I was more than a little nervous, for two reasons: After that last tour, I knew I was quite capable of losing my temper, and the same could be said of my self-taught-the-hard-way managing director.

"Come after 7 p.m.," Mangas had told me on the phone, his voice soft and tired. Resigned, even. Indeed, when I sat down at his ever-impressive oak desk, I couldn't help noticing that something had changed about him. He looked at me differently, with something in his eyes resembling genuine interest. It made me glance away awkwardly, my eyes automatically seeking out the familiar sign above his desk. But it was gone. No more *New Management Directive: No Work? Fired!*

"My boy, I owe you an apology," Mangas began, again in that soft, resigned voice. "I kept you waiting for weeks and weeks this winter without paying you a penny. And then, when the tours started, I underpaid you. There was no insurance either – good thing nothing happened on the road."

I was too baffled to speak.

"Anyway, all of that doesn't matter anymore. We've gone bankrupt. We're bust. Out of business. Lambros Mangas will have to pull himself out of the big mess he made ... yet again."

"I'm sorry to hear that..." I managed to say after a while. But he held up his hand. "Please. Not a word. It is I who is truly,

truly sorry. The only thing that comforts me in all of this is that I know you did a good job. You survived. Ancient Corinth… I heard about your undercover work there – the tour guides union called. And believe me, I defended you. And apologized to them, too. I know it was wrong of me to ask that of you. If only you had told me you'd never been there before…"

I shrugged. "Not to worry. Throw me into the pool and I'll swim."

Mangas suddenly banged his hand on the table. "I KNEW it! I knew it when I first saw you! With that humongous umbrella of yours. I told myself: Here is a young man who wants to see the world! And you haven't let me down – never mind that scam of a letter I received from this asshole here, this Mister Provo—"

"Provoost."

"Yes, him. Look. Whatever happened on that tour, and whatever he accuses me of… I know none of it was your fault. It was I who put you in these situations, but in the end you came out on top! I remember you told me you never did your military service. I think you have now. Yes, now you really have."

And with that, he opened a drawer and pulled out a fat paper envelope he handed over to me with a nod. "The money I owe you, money I didn't pay for insurance. For your hours at the office, your days on the road. Go have a nice summer now, my boy. With your *wife*, of course."

We shook hands warmly, and then he wrapped me in the biggest bear hug.

The end.

Curtains.

Music.

Violins.

All's well that ends well.

Except, of course, that is not what really happened.

As soon as I returned from that disastrous final tour, Mangas was already on the phone to me, explaining that as the summer season had now begun there'd be no more tours. They would only resume in September, once the worst of the summer heat was over. But September seemed lightyears away to me at that point.

Needless to say, the sign on his office wall hadn't changed either: *No work? Fired!*

I didn't hear from him for the next three months, and when he did reach out, it was through his assistant. By then, I was no longer living in Athens, but still he had tracked me down. It was the end of September, and new SolAir tours were scheduled. Was I available?

I told him that I had found other work since we'd last spoken and wasn't planning to return to Athens anytime soon.

And so it was. In the interim, I had become a tour guide on the island of Chios.

Part II
The Self-Made Hostess Handbook

*Note to the reader: For reasons which will become apparent very soon, in this part of the story a tour leader, tour guide or "holiday rep" will be referred to as a **hostess**, regardless of gender.*

1. Fucking Around

***Excerpt from* The Self-Made Hostess Handbook*:**

"If you want to work as a hostess, and if you want your boss, colleagues and guests to respect you, follow rule number one: Make sure you are always there for them when they need you. Be punctual, always.

Rule number two follows swiftly on rule number one: No matter the circumstances, always give the impression of being in control. That means, don't just be punctual – be there and show that you want to be there."

"Wanted: Tour leader on Chios. Perfect German required," the ad in *Athens News* read. It had only been a week since my career as a SolAir tour guide had hit rock bottom, on that overnight ferry from Santorini to Crete. I was unemployed again, so what did I have to lose? I found Chios on a map: a large island very close to Turkey. Nobody I asked seemed to know very much about it. Then I went to a secondhand bookshop in Monastiraki and bought an old German textbook hoping it might trigger the recall of my secondary school German skills. Sure, Dutch and German have many similarities, but like so many Dutchmen I couldn't do much more than bluff my way into German. Fortunately, the grammar from that textbook did ring a bell. So I cleared my throat and made the call.

That same afternoon I entered the spacious office of Frau Uschi, a bigshot at Plotin Travel, then the number-one incoming tour operator in Greece. It turned out that Plotin also represented a number of smaller tour operators on the islands, one of which was Chios Travel, where they so badly needed that fluent Germanophone. How badly exactly? Very badly, apparently, for after exchanging a few niceties with Uschi in my rusty German, she offered me the job right away – including an attractive salary, a free apartment in the main town of Chios and a moped for my unlimited use. In other words: Chios Tours was desperate for anyone who could say *Guten Morgen* without blinking an eye. Also, could I *bitte sehr* bring along some passport photos tomorrow so Plotin's HR department could arrange a work permit for me?

What a marvelous display of efficiency! A work permit was still something of an achievement in early-nineties Greece. I'd heard countless stories of people who'd had to stand in line for weeks just to obtain one. But Frau Uschi got me my permit in no time – along with a one-way ticket by plane to Chios. She told me that my new boss's name was Alex, the managing director of Chios Travel, and with a thin smile she added, "Half the island calls him *The Prince*, the other half prefers *The Snake.*"

I wasn't in the least concerned. All I knew was that I had just escaped a sticky, sweltering summer in Athens and would, instead, be on a Greek island until October. And moreover, I knew that when I boarded the plane to Chios with work permit in hand, I'd be literally leaving behind those chaotic days with Mangas Travel.

My first views of Chios from above were more than promising: beaches, forests, mountain villages and endless orchards of lemon and orange trees. The moment I stepped off the plane, the scent of all those citrus trees almost swept me off my feet. Then a pretty young woman appeared – radiant smile, wild black curls blowing in the wind – and held up a sign with my name on it. She welcomed me with two kisses on the cheek. "Hiya!" she said in an American accent. "I am Kali, your new colleague. I am, like, *so happy* you're here."

"Are you from the US?" I asked her, somewhat clumsily.

Kali shook her head vigorously. "*Ooooochi, vre*! No way! I was born right here! I studied marketing in San Diego a couple of years back, but that's about it."

In the car, Kali gave me the first hint at my job description, saying it would include a mix of excursions and what she called *hostessing*. Hostessing? She gave me a sweet smile. "Sorry. It's *holiday rep*, I know. Your predecessor was a girl. Anyway, Alex calls everyone a hostess here, even the Norwegian Viking-type-of-guy we have at the office."

So I would be a hostess. Would I start work right away? Kali tapped me on the upper leg. "All you're supposed to do in the next couple of days is read up on everything. Your first airport transfer is at the end of the week. A bunch of Swiss people. Ah yes, and Alex wants to meet you, too. Tonight, 6 p.m."

She then drove me to the most expensive hotel in town, the Chandris, which dominated the sizable port. The Chandris Hotel had a 1960s-style of luxury about it that I immediately liked. It felt like at any moment Sean Connery would enter the lobby and introduce himself as Bond, James Bond. Kali exchanged a few words with the receptionist and blew me a kiss as she was leaving. "See you at the office!"

Going up to my room, I was surprised how smoothly the noiseless elevator took me to the highest floor. Efficiency! When I opened the door to my room, the first thing that struck me was the panoramic view overlooking Chios Town. I could hardly believe this was real. Look at the king-size bed, the elegant leather sofa next to it, the larger-than-life jacuzzi… I turned on the gold-coloured taps and emptied a lilac bottle of bubble bath into the piping hot water. Everything was coming up roses.

The office of Chios Travel was as modern as any in Athens. Kali was waiting for me, leaning in the doorway looking every inch the California girl in her sleeveless, ochre-colored dress. Her eyes lit up when she saw me approach. She stroked my cheek for a few seconds and closed her eyes: "Jasmine?" she asked. Then without moving away, for we were standing only a few inches apart, she pressed a pile of travel brochures at me. "You can read those here," she said. "It's quiet this afternoon. Everyone else is out doing their visiting hours." Her eyes were gleaming, and for a second, I thought she might kiss me, Hollywood style. A loose strand of her curls brushed against my lips and nose, a nose that was already struggling with all the pollen on the island. I turned away as a prolonged sneezing fit gripped me. That was Kali's cue to take a chair behind a desk halfway across the room, the one most centrally located in the office. She picked up the phone and was almost immediately busy scolding someone for having double-booked a bunch of hotel rooms.

I looked around. Plenty of empty desks here. But I'd only seen a glimpse of Chios and wanted to try out that moped. Was Kali ok with that?

"Fine by me," she smiled, professionally. "Just don't forget the boss wants to see you at 6 p.m.!"

The moped in question turned out to be a reliable 1975 Yamaha Townmate that had been upgraded with a 125cc engine. Soon enough, I was riding through the impressive mountains of the Chian hinterlands – all pine forests and forgotten monasteries. An intoxicating mix of smells, sights and sounds overwhelmed me. Unexpectedly, the mountains gave way to a majestic view over the west coast of Chios. It was breathtaking: ridge after ridge, hazy shades of brown that gradually melted into the turquoise of the Aegean Sea. This was it. This was the Greece I had wanted to experience! Right below me I could see a bay with a pristine white beach. A few minutes later, I was riding toward it through a dry riverbed along the olive trees. The Blue Lagoon, for me alone. After a wonderful swim, I opened my first German travel guide to the island and soon fell asleep.

When I woke, it was almost half past five. Oops. I shouldn't keep my new boss waiting on my first day – otherwise, I feared The Prince might turn into The Snake. I hopped on my moped and started back in the direction of the town, passing dozens of other heavenly beaches along the way. I glanced at my watch: I could just make the 6 o'clock appointment. Without warning, however, my bike started losing speed. I tried to accelerate, but the engine hardly responded. I got off the moped, lifted the saddle and peered inside the small tank. There was hardly any gasoline left.

Clearly, this remote road was not the place where helpful tourists or islanders might pass at any minute. I had no other option but to start walking, though there was not a village in sight, nor even a single house. Luckily, within a few minutes of walking, a canary-yellow truck appeared. This was going to be my salvation! I stood in the middle of the road; if the driver wanted to press on, it would have to be over my dead body.

The truck stopped well ahead of me. Behind the wheel was a young guy, not a truck driver type at all. In fact, he seemed more like a lost student, and bore an uncanny likeness to a young Woody Allen. He kindly offered to drive me to the next village. On the way, he asked me where I had come from and how I had ended up all the way out here, well off the beaten track. I swallowed and said, "Uh, I'm on holiday, visiting a friend who works here." Young Woody nodded silently, then launched into an expert discourse on the island. The history of Chios, the economy, the art, famous Chians, politicians, shipbuilders, painters... more than enough material to cover all my upcoming tours. It turned out that young Woody had just graduated with a degree in political science – just like me, though I decided to keep that information to myself.

The winding road we were on ran through a forest of pine trees. After about 7 or 8 kilometers, we reached the small village of Vessa. It had the feel of a forgotten outpost, with its collection of derelict stone houses and its one *kafeníon* under an age-old plane tree. Some listless men in overalls were seated on a bench, contemplating the truck that had disturbed their afternoon slumber. Young Woody leaped down from the cabin, conferred with the men and pointed at me. One of them stood and walked away from our group very slowly. I glanced at the dashboard clock: I was officially late. Would the Prince appreciate a good story?

Eventually the man reappeared, carrying a large jerrycan half full of gasoline. He handed it to me indifferently. I waved a 500-drachmae note in his direction, but this caused all the men to get up, shouting in unison "Ochi, ochi!" and shaking their heads vehemently.

On the way back, young Woody gave me a piece of advice. "On this island, it is best to keep a safe distance from everybody. Otherwise, before you know it, you'll be in some sort of intrigue and you will never get rid of it again."

"Rid of the intrigue?" I asked.

"Rid of the island and its people," he mumbled.

I was grateful and relieved to have arrived at a place where kindness was still the norm. Then it dawned on me that I was no longer a traveler: I would be working at a fixed place, with a fixed apartment and fixed working hours. If I wanted to last longer than a few days here, I'd have to be available. Reliable. *There.*

With the tank half full, I headed back up the road into the mountains, through the forest and toward the lights of Chios Town. I finally stumbled into the office just before closing time, almost two hours late, windswept and bleary-eyed. Kali was still the only one there. I dropped any attempt to make light of my late arrival when I saw the stern look on her face. "The boss wants to see you," was all she said, and pointed me to a room in the back.

The door was half open but I knocked all the same. No answer. I entered the dimly lit area and saw a man sitting behind an enormous desk. Alex. The Prince. Although he couldn't have been older than forty, he was almost completely bald, apart from some grey plucks of hair above his ears. Judging from his sharp facial features, I could see why some people called him The Snake. It wouldn't have surprised me if a long, thin tongue had struck out at me from within that sharp face.

He looked up. "Ah, yes," he said in an all-too-measured tone, "Our new Dutchman from Athens." He ignored my outstretched hand, rested both palms flat on his desk, elbows out, and suddenly roared at me. "Where have you been? Fucking around on day one, huh?! I was just about to book your ticket back to Athens – at *your* expense."

From that day on, I was always, always *there*.

2. Asterix in Helvetia

Excerpt from* The Self-Made Hostess Handbook*:

*"When carrying out an **airport transfer**, the hostess must ensure that he is clearly visible in the arrivals hall. Furthermore, it is imperative he look fresh, well-groomed and, indeed, radiate that special holiday vibe, keeping his travel company's logo at shoulder height. The transfer bus should be easy to spot from his position, so that he can send the arriving guests straight to it. The bus driver, likewise appropriately dressed, should involve himself in his main task: the loading of guests' luggage onto the bus, briskly and efficiently. Once the hostess has met and ticked all guests off his list, he too should board the bus, then count all heads in a discreet manner from front to back, and once more, back to front. Only then should he signal to the driver to start the engine and head toward their hotels."*

Chios Airport was a tiny affair, with a runway too short for the latest generation of charter aircraft. With international tourism to the island still in its infancy, the month of June saw the arrival of no more than one plane per day. Today's happy band of travelers were arriving from Zurich. I was told to pick up a group who had booked with the Greek-Swiss tour operator Matterhorn Tours. It was my first airport transfer, and The Prince had riled me up with one simple phrase: "We're gonna make you a *hostess!*"

I had taken Kali aside. "I just want to make sure that he knows that *hostess* is female, right?"

She shot me the kind of cold look she'd been giving me ever since I had been so dreadfully late to meet The Prince on my first day. "Don't you dare correct him!"

As soon as I saw the plane from Zurich touch the ground at Chios Airport, I positioned myself at the building exit, next to the hostess of another Swiss travel company called ESCO. Her name was Greta, a cheerful girl from Lucerne. When I didn't immediately understand her Swiss-German accent, she switched to English – just what my self-confidence needed. I glanced again at the sheet of paper on which I'd scribbled some opening lines, *Guten Morgen, wie war Ihr Flug?* and such. Hopefully that would get me past the first minutes of communication.

The bus driver I was to work with that day was called Lakis. Tall, good-looking, and somewhere in his forties, he seemed to have a jokester side to him. When he discovered that my Greek wasn't yet up to par, he began teaching me some of the local dialect's four-letter words, effectively scrambling all the pre-arranged sentences I had prepared in German for my arriving guests. I showed him my Greek Asterix comic book to prove that I was truly trying to improve my Greek, only to have it snatched from my hands. With a satisfied smirk, Lakis took up his position at the front of the bus, enjoying every detail of *Asterix and the Olympic Games*.

Sooner than expected, the guests emerged from the makeshift passport check. Greta's ESCO sign went up. I hastily checked myself in a car mirror. A gust of wind had blown my hair in all directions and the blue shirt I had on was obviously meant for jogging – but blue was the color of Matterhorn Tours. "What do you mean you don't have a blue tie? You're a hostess now!" The Prince had hissed at me earlier that morning, his reptilian demeanor winning the upper hand once again. "I am happy to wear a blue shirt, if you want," I had told him, "but you can forget about the tie."

"Fucking stubborn Dutchman," The Prince had mumbled. But I knew he wasn't going to send me back to Athens. The Swiss tour operator had been complaining for weeks: "Where is our German-speaking guide? Who will take care of our *liebe Kunden*?"

When I looked through my passenger list, I couldn't help thinking of Asterix, and not just because I'd been reading it earlier that morning. The list of names indicated Aeberlix 2 PAX, Muellix 2 PAX, Delmanox 1 PAX, and so on. "PAX" stood for persons, that much I knew. But what puzzled me was why every one of my ten Swiss travelers seemed to have a surname that ended in "x". There was, however, no time to wonder about that now.

I quickly held up the Matterhorn Tours sign. A crowd moved directly toward Greta and she expertly handled her forty or so guests. I understood little of what I heard: *Joa yo, Esco, grütsi, muesli, pletznimn, yo yo ya*... Oops, there was someone looking my way. Keep the sign up, and keep smiling. Eye contact. Clear the throat.

"Guten Morgen."

"Grütsi."

"Uh... Ihr Name?"

"Aeberli. Hotel Xenios."

"Ah yes, here. Aeberlix, ja?"

"Neeh, neeh, Ae-ber-lì."

I finally saw it: Aeberlix, Muellix and Delmanox had no x at the end of their names. Kali had typed the *x 2 PAX* so close behind the names that she had unknowingly recreated half the inhabitants of Asterix and Obelix's Gaul village in my head. *Aeberlix 2 PAX* should be *Aeberli x 2 PAX*. I drew a vertical line to the left of all x-es.

Next was Ms. Delmano, an attractive lady dressed in the shortest of skirts.

"Grütsi," I smiled.

"Buon Giorno."

Oh no! Maybe she spoke some French? But she didn't understand much of that either. So I just pointed to the bus, whereupon she said, "Ah, il bus."

Lakis could not suppress a grin when we were finally all on board. "It took you quite a while to get that small handful of people on the bus," he said.

When I showed him the list of Asterix and Obelix's compatriots, he collapsed with laughter. He then mimicked Obelix impeccably: "Those Helvetians are crazy!"

It was the beginning of a beautiful friendship between tour bus driver and hostess.

3. The Evil Eye

***Excerpt from* The Self-Made Hostess Handbook*:**

*"At the **welcome drink**, the hostess should relay to the guests all practical information pertaining to their stay on the island: the local currency, the local electrical voltage and the local bus schedule; doctors, dentists, and the local attitude toward topless sunbathing; the hostess's visiting hours and the breakfast times. Last but not least, the hostess should mention that his guests are welcome to arrange a car or moped rental, as well as excursions on the island – but would be wise to do so through the hostess directly. While guests are free to embark on any excursion or vehicle rental of their choosing, advise them that booking through the hostess is rather a guarantee, as a car or moped booked through the hostess will be reliable and any excursion certain to actually occur. It is for this reason vital for the hostess to come across as reliable. As someone who knows the place. As someone they can depend upon so far from home."*

Four Helvetians had taken the trouble to attend my first *Willkommstriff*. The Heini couple wasn't a surprise, but I had not expected Ms. Delmano, who was positively gorgeous in her low-cut bathing suit. The French-speaking Mr. Vervié was also there: big, fat, bald and armed with a malicious stare. Four people, three languages – Switzerland in a nutshell. *"Deutsch ist auch kein problem,"* Vervié offered, the only one who ordered ouzo instead of orange juice. Heaving and sighing, he brought the full glass up to his mouth and emptied it in one go.

Look out, here's Mr. Bottoms Up. This man had probably been drunk from the moment he set foot on the plane.

"Please tell me, *Herr Reiseleiter*, about that sign for the gift shop at the hotel entrance. They don't sell poison there, do they? Or don't you know that *gift* in German means *poison*? Hahahaha!"

I was in the middle of a difficult moment, trying to explain *Büsse, Strom, Telefon* and such things to the guests, but that didn't stop Vervié from cutting in, which threw me off and made my already shabby German even shabbier. When I managed to answer him in reasonable French, he urged me to leave my attempts at German aside. He turned to the Heini's, "You understand *Französisch,* don't you?"

"Eh, neeh, hardly," was their response.

"*Mon Dieu!*" he exclaimed, raising his hands to the heavens.

So I continued hacking away in German, through an increasingly erratic narration. How on earth was I going to put an end to this ordeal? I pressed on to the part about car rentals and excursions and hoped I'd be out of there soon.

"Excursions? Doesn't interest me a bit, *Herr Reiseleiter.*" Vervié decided that it had been enough; he got up and walked toward the hotel bar, very unsteadily. I hastily asked the Heini's if they had any further questions. No, thank you, everything was clear. Then Ms. Delmano rested her perfectly manicured hand on my arm for a moment and asked me a question. I briefly wondered if I'd gone crazy, for although she spoke Italian, I heard her clearly utter the Dutch slang word for testicles, *kloten.* "Kloten?" I echoed automatically. Then she showed me her plane ticket, and it dawned on me that Kloten also happened to be the original name of the Zurich Airport. I don't think Ms. Delmano understood why I broke into a fit of nervous laughter, but, not in the least perturbed, she proceeded to book a boat excursion. That meant my first commission: 10 percent of the excursion price minus a few vague taxes (mainly for the benefit of The Prince's wallet), so in the end what remained would be roughly enough for a cappuccino.

As I was finally preparing to leave the hotel, I noticed Vervié raising a stink at reception. He caught sight of me and loudly called me over: "Ah! *Herr Reiseleiter! Kommen Sie mal!*" He was in the company of the hotel manager, a young Greek-American man looking rather desperate. Vervié turned to me, fuming in indignant German, "This has never happened to me before! In all my years, I have never once had to pay for a hotel safe. *Niemals!* There is nothing, NOTHING about it in the travel brochure!"

Somewhere in the back of my brain, self-taught-the-hard-way Mangas was signaling to me: "Keep smiling!" The hotel manager informed me in English that all the hotels on the island charged an added fee for the use of the safes. I asked him to continue in Greek, which he did, adding, "Tell the guy that he is talking bullshit!"

"Sir, it's standard here—" I started.

"*Quatsch!*" Vervié exploded. "I demand that you show me your company's contract with this hotel, right now!"

The hotel manager was getting increasingly pissed off. The quarrel had been going on for quite some time and now his integrity was being called into question. He went in search of the contract. "Come and see, sir!"

I followed them into the office, where the hotel manager began to explain once again, waving the contract in the air, that safes had never been included in any deal, and that the hotel could determine the price itself.

"Then they should have said so in Switzerland!" Vervié interrupted. He turned to me again, "I will write a letter to Matterhorn Tours!"

"Yes," the manager snapped in Greek, "let the *malákas* write."

"What does the *salopard* say?" Vervié asked me.

"Best write a letter to Zurich. It is not the fault of the hotel."

Vervié's small, malicious eyes slid from the hotel manager to me. He turned red and burst into a mighty series of coughs. Finally, he spun on his heels and strode away from us with a surprisingly steady gait.

As I left the hotel, I realized that this was only day one of Mr Vervié's three-week stay on the island. And I would probably have to face him every day.

But it wouldn't come to that. The next morning, while I was busy leading my first excursion off the island to neighboring Turkey, Vervié received a telegram notifying him his father had suddenly passed away. He called the Chios Travel office straightaway, cursing everything and everyone, until they arranged an outrageously expensive ticket for him back to

Zurich. When Kali told me the whole story that same evening, she gave me a kind of quizzical look and asked, out of the blue, "Were you by any chance born on a Saturday?"

I already knew what was going to come, and said, "As a matter of fact, I was."

She grew anxious. "My goodness! Christòs kai Panagyìa! Blue eyes, born on a Saturday… you, you gave Vervié the evil eye!"

She hastily made the sign of a cross and spat on the office floor right in front of me.

4. A Mind Like a *Sieb*

***Excerpt from* The Self-Made Hostess Handbook:**

"The hostess must make himself available during specified hours at the hotels where his guests are staying in order to provide support. These visiting hours should occur at least twice but preferably three times a week. The host must locate himself in the immediate vicinity of a poster-sized information board, placed in a clearly visible spot in the lobby and identified by the logo of the organization for which he works. It should list pertinent schedules, including the departure times of the charter planes, while maintaining an overall spirit that is light and casual. The board should also include photographs of local sites interspersed with the latest updates on exciting excursions, handwritten in marker and with plenty of exclamation marks to impart a feeling of welcome and anticipation.

During visiting hours (which should more accurately be called visiting half hours), guests have the opportunity to divulge how their holidays are going. These types of interactions

"Say, you wouldn't have some more cutlery for us, would you? We booked a studio with kitchenette, and all we found in the cupboard were two crooked forks. Mr. Thodoros brought us some knives and spoons, but it's all a little... spartan for us. A little *unheimisch*, if you know what we mean. For example, we could really use a *sieb*."

On Chios, the complaints I received from guests were almost exclusively grievances about the hotels where they were staying. Some hotels had minor issues and responsible owners who were willing to fix them. The Hotel Perivoli was one such, where I popped over twice a week for my visiting hours with a peaceful, easy feeling. If there was ever the slightest problem, like a wooden floor that creaked, it could be quickly solved with a bit of help from the owner, Panos. Visiting hours at the Hotel Summer Sun were more difficult, however, as the hotel kept experiencing major difficulties that I could do little to fix. One fine day, the Summer Sun's heating system went down, leaving no hot water for its eighty residents, and it would take two weeks for the few replacement parts to arrive from Athens, by which time most of the guests would have already returned home. But invariably, the visiting hours I dreaded most were those at the Sea View Hotel, owned by Thodoros. Here was a manager who cared very little for what the tourism sector calls "the quality of the experience." And it was here that my guests found their kitchen supplied with only those two crooked forks.

While Thodoros apparently didn't care much for cutlery, what was worse was his decision to rent out a number of the studios to several Russian girls who worked in what the Rough Guide described as "Chios' tiny red-light district." Initially, the girls used their studios for sleeping purposes only, but when they started receiving clients in their rooms, my Swiss guests were less than pleased. A river of complaints started flooding in, which if even half were true meant Thodoros was running a Wild West saloon instead of an island hotel. The Prince agreed with me: the girls had to go. Thodoros didn't dare go against him, so he moved them out, eventually finding the girls new rooms in a hotel aptly named the Welcome House, right in the middle of the tiny red-light district.

Still, Thodoros remained a tough nut to crack. Over the winter he had signed contracts with a number of European tour operators, making the most of his "sea view". The photos that subsequently appeared in various German, Swiss and Austrian travel brochures testified to panoramic views over the bay of Agia Pelagia. Upon arrival, however, the guests beheld something different: the sea now completely hidden from view by the construction of a new building, the Blue Wave Studios, which had been built in record time that Easter. The owner? None other than Thodoros himself.

I tried moving some of my guests from the Sea View Hotel to the Blue Wave Studios, but Thodoros was an expert at sidestepping me. Raising his hands in mock despair, he argued, "Listen, my friend, all those rooms are already rented out to English guests, and I can't keep moving them back and forth!" Once more, The Prince intervened and informed him that the lack of the promised sea view was legal grounds for a serious refund – for which Thodoros himself would be liable. Thodoros ultimately complied, but not without some muttering and cursing. To his mind, he was a taverna owner who'd happened to own a piece of land by the seaside that he had filled with studios. Now that the studios were there, the guests could fend for themselves. If they wanted to see the sea, the beach was only a fifty-meter stroll away. He was busy enough with his taverna.

Sieb. I didn't know what it meant, and the friendly Swiss couple did not know the word in English. Apparently, it was a utensil they needed for cooking pasta. After some miming and gesturing I got it: a sieve, of course! I routed out Thodoros, who was making a show of being busy in his taverna kitchen. He didn't know what I meant by sieve, or *sieb*, nor did I know the word for it in Greek. Another round of pantomime did the trick.

"What the hell do they want a sieve for?" he sighed. "They can get a *makaronada* for just a few of their Swiss francs here in the taverna!" Eventually, he rummaged in a large wooden closet and pulled out a massive sieve that could have handled at least ten kilos of spaghetti. And by the looks of it, it hadn't been used in over a century. When I presented it to my guests, they were too taken aback to ask for a smaller one.

All in all, visiting hours were my least favorite activity in my time as a hostess. Besides the issues that Thodoros caused, the complaints included pool water that was either too hot or too cold, rude hotel staff who always served the meals lukewarm, and excessive noise from the hotel bar at night. All of which required proper follow up: I had to bring these matters up variously with the hotel manager, Kali or The Prince. Failure to do so would result in bitter, long, drawn-out complaints... about me.

Inevitably, it did all once go terribly wrong – and where else but at Thodoros' Sea View Hotel? It concerned the case of Anja Müller from Basel, a tall blonde of around forty years old. She had just undergone a very hard divorce and was in desperate need of some peace and quiet on a remote Greek island where the sun was always shining.

On one of her first days, returning to her hotel room from a day at the beach with her five-year-old son Heini, she saw preparations being made for a party by the pool. At 8 p.m., the large speakers commenced pumping out loud dance beats. By midnight the noise had not stopped, and at 3 a.m. it was still going strong. Heini tossed and turned restlessly in his bed, while his mother lay staring at the ceiling. The next morning at breakfast, Anja Müller rounded up a number of the other sleepless guests. Another of the hostesses came by for her visiting hour, listened to the guests' complaints and went to speak to Thodoros. He shrugged his shoulders as only Thodoros could: He had booked a series of weddings for the summer months and was not going to just cancel them. The hostess insisted, and her guests were relocated to another part of the building further away from the noise.

But for Anja Müller, nothing changed. She checked the information boards to find that *her* hostess would not be coming by again until Wednesday, which meant four more nights of misery. She called the Chios Travel office and was informed that her hostess was in Turkey that day. The next pool party was on Monday: a bachelor party that didn't end until Tuesday around noon. While Anja Müller and Heini were having their breakfast after another sleepless night, a bunch of fully clothed and completely plastered partygoers were still frolicking in the adjacent hotel pool. Little Heini, at this point, hadn't slept more than ten hours altogether since they'd arrived. He just wanted to go home.

And his mum? She shuffled through the hotel like a zombie, pouring her sorrows out to other guests who had been lucky enough to be staying on the quiet side of the building. She struck up a friendship with a nice family, but this well-rested, happy couple and their cheerful kids inadvertently made her own situation even more poignant. On Tuesday, she called Chios Travel again and demanded to speak to the hostess. "Sorry, your hostess is in Turkey today." Again? What kind of service was this? Was she completely left to her own devices?

On Tuesday night, the first night since her arrival with no party at the hotel, she slept reasonably well. But one look at the event board at the front desk showed there'd be new parties from Thursday onwards. To make matters worse, Heini had injured himself on one of the underwater lamps that had been placed inside the pool solely to add ambience to the night parties. She was ready, in short, to demand a total refund and never set foot on the island of Chios again.

According to the information board, her hostess's visiting hour was set for that Wednesday from 6:30 to 7:00 p.m. She was already waiting by the board at a quarter past six. At a little over a half hour later, I sauntered into the lobby, looking suspiciously like I'd just had a swim. I greeted the girls at reception and quickly scanned the room. Anja Müller got up and approached me.

"Are you the *Reiseleiter* who was in Turkey all this time?"

I was startled by her loud tone, "Ehm, not all this time... Please, let's sit down."

She did not sit down, and instead started recounting her whole story: all that was wrong with the hotel; lots about her own personal situation; some about her son, as well. My expression registered astonishment, then became more and more blank as her narration progressed. She could tell I didn't understand her German very well, even though she did her best to speak Hochdeutsch.

"Yes, I understand," I began, though it was obvious she did not think I did, "I understand that you fault me for not being here, but I did not receive any messages, neither on Saturday nor yesterday. As for your complaint, I will speak to Mister Thodoros."

I could only imagine what she must have been thinking of me. Look at this young man, touring around on his motorbike, smiling at girls on the beach while letting his guests sink into the swamp! He didn't even bother to shower after his swim – look at the salt water dried on his skin!

"*Hör mal zu*, you have to understand that I haven't slept a wink in five nights! I've waited long enough. Let me show you something." She showed me where the pool was and then pointed at her room, directly above it. It was the first time I had really taken in the layout of the hotel beyond the reception area.

"Hm, yes. You—you know what?" I stammered. "Tonight I'll talk to my boss, and if you can meet me here tomorrow morning at 8:30, we'll get you a quieter room."

She told me again how important it was that they sleep well – little Heini had developed bags under his eyes from the fatigue. Could she be sure that I would do something for her?

"I assure you, tomorrow everything will be all right."

Anja Müller was downstairs by a quarter past eight the next morning. The lobby was crowded with a large group waiting for an excursion bus. She recognized the happy family she had befriended among the guests. They greeted her kindly. "We're going on the South Chios excursion. Our *Reiseleiter* is the one in charge, you know, that Dutchman."

That surprised her. "What time does the bus come then?"

"At 8:30."

When the bus pulled in, ten minutes behind schedule, Anja Müller watched me step off it to collect everyone's tour receipts. When the last of the group had boarded, I took a hasty glance in the direction of the hotel. All the guests were on the bus, everything was ok.

"I'm terribly sorry. I have no excuse. I completely forgot. We were already delayed, and I was in a hurry."

"Come on now! You wouldn't have had time anyway."

"Yes. I could have arranged everything in a few minutes."

"Ah, *quatsch*! With a bus full of people waiting? Why didn't you tell me you had another job to do? You just left me here. On purpose."

The word Anja Müller used was *absichtlich*: intentionally. I didn't know the word then, but I understood very well what she meant. It wasn't true, but then again it wasn't entirely untrue either. I had let her down badly, and I didn't know what to say or do to make it up to her.

Then an idea struck me, of the kind Mangas had tried on me back in Athens. It was a bit of a gamble but I had no other options left: "Maybe you'd like to come along on the South Chios excursion for free?"

"Well, how would that make things better? We just want to go home..."

Anja Müller finally agreed to the free excursion, after I had negotiated a better room for her, of course, which Thodoros described as *absolutely really very quiet, my friend*.

Meanwhile, at the office, another epic conflict was unfolding between The Prince and Thodoros. Over the past weeks, hordes of other hotel guests had complained to their hostesses, too, of the nightly pool extravaganzas. My colleagues were getting tired of being the scapegoats. Now The Prince had a hostess insurrection to face as well. Considering the growing possibility of massive refunds that would ruin both Thodoros and The Prince in one fell swoop, The Prince was forced to take action. "Listen to me!" he roared over the phone. "Cut those damn parties or I rebook everybody to the Golden fucking Beach! What was that you said, maláka?! Do you want to stay closed next year? And the following years as well?"

Thodoros had no choice but to give in. The Prince held his royal title for a reason.

A few days later, Anja Müller and her son were in the lobby, when our tour bus pulled up at exactly half past eight. I risked a look in her direction and could see right away that a lot had improved. Anja looked positively radiant in a light blue dress and a Berlin 1920's–style hat. Driver Lakis, who was aware of the Anja Müller saga, gave me a wink and said, "Let's make this trip worth her while."

On the excursion, I got to know Anja, as I now called her, a lot better. She was the only single parent on board – in fact, she was the only single person I'd seen on this excursion in a while. At our first coffee break, Anja hesitated for a moment when she saw all the couples seated at their tables for two. Lakis stepped in, and it was here that I started to understand what he had meant by making it "worth her while". He called Anja over to our table and proceeded cheerily to engage her and Heini in conversation. The boy lit up like a flame. During lunch at the next stop, Lakis arranged for the taverna owner to bring out a few extra plates for them, plus three glasses of homemade ouzo. By lunchtime, Lakis had them both eating out of the palm of his hand. He had bought a bottle of local wine for Anja and some sweets for Heini (which Anja normally wouldn't allow him to eat, at least not all at once, as he did during that lunch with a big guilty smile). As the day continued, Lakis horsed around with the kid, while graciously helping Anja in and out of the bus. By the time we arrived at the beach for an afternoon swim, Anja was having the time of her life. Lakis even went as far as doing something no Greek tour bus driver ever does in public: he went out for a swim with Heini.

As Anja sat next to me on my beach towel, with her pretty dress, blonde curls and red cheeks, she asked if Lakis was married. I said he was. She smiled and shook her head. Then unexpectedly she put a hand on my shoulder. "You're a nice young man," she said. "You love this country, I can tell. But you're not fit to do this job. You really are too absent-minded. You have a mind like a *sieb*."

Part III

Day-tripping on Chios

Lena, the tall German hostess with the short fuse, refused to believe what the baker's daughter had just told her: "What do you mean, Nikos, your oven *kaputt*? There are eighty people sitting there waiting for their food, *ja*? You think they want cold meatballs?"

By then, however, the damage had already been done: Eighty people, seated at ten long tables in the village square, had just been served ice cold *keftedes*. While the bouzouki band played on, while the baker's children served a round of free ouzo to the eighty guests, all of whom were shoving their inedible keftedes aside, Nikos was crouched behind the bakery oven, fiddling with a bunch of cables. There was no other taverna in the village, let alone another good oven capable of feeding so many. There was nothing to hope for except this bakery oven, which had just broken down.

Welcome to the first Greek Night of the season, an idea concocted by The Prince. Chios Travel had deals with tour operators from Norway, Holland, the UK, Germany and Switzerland. These companies were all represented *in situ* by holiday reps – or as The Prince, and by now everyone else, called them, *hostesses*. The Prince was the main incoming tour operator on the island: He provided the hostesses with office space, and he was the one to get on the phone in case of trouble with the hotels, which was often enough. In turn, each of the hostesses recruited guests for the island excursions and guided the tour on the bus themselves. On any given week, you could book the South Chios excursion in Norwegian, English,

Dutch or German narration. The Prince would provide the same bus and the same driver, who would take the same route on the same schedule each time, and only the person guiding the tour would change, a hostess speaking his or her language for guests from his or her language zone.

My position as a hostess was a little different from that of my fellow hostesses, who all had been recruited in their countries of origin, and then sent out to Chios as part of a contract between their outgoing tour operators (TUI, for example) and The Prince. There was only one outgoing tour operator who had not included a hostess in its contract with The Prince: the Swiss company Matterhorn Tours. That's where I came in, after spotting that job ad for a "tour leader with perfect German" back in Athens. My Norwegian, British and Dutch colleagues worked solely for their companies at home, but I had arrived on Chios via the local Greek route, with my one-and-only boss The Prince. So whenever there was trouble on the island, either with a hotel or with Chios Travel itself, the other hostesses had a much stronger position to negotiate from than I had. They could, for example, refuse any attempt by The Prince to put twenty Germans and twenty Norwegians together on one bus – their companies' contracts specified excursions in their language *exclusively*. As for me, on top of my German-speaking guests, I would receive assorted tourists who'd signed up for excursions through Chios Travel directly – Greeks, Francophones, and even the odd Israeli. It was then up to me to juggle the languages to everyone's satisfaction (the Israeli spoke fluent English, thank god).

As if this wasn't complicated enough, Lena, the German hostess with the short fuse, had no time for leading the bus tours. Being the only German TUI representative on the island, she had to cater to more than half the tourists on Chios at any given moment. TUI had made a deal with The Prince: It would be his responsibility to provide the German TUI guests with a guide on the bus, and that guide happened to be me. So whenever The Prince decided to squeeze a Greek family onto my German bus, he ran three risks: He would force me to do the tour in simultaneous German and Greek, which would easily turn my efforts into a linguistic mess. He would also risk complaints from the German travelers, who had been promised a tour in German and German only. And last but not least, he ran the risk of complaints from the unfortunate Greek family – and if there was one country that had made complaining into an art form, it was without a doubt the Hellenic Republic.

The Prince didn't listen to my worries: I was sufficiently capable of dealing with a few grumpy faces, wasn't I? And after all, didn't I get handsomely paid for these excursions? That part, I had to admit, was true. On top of a basic hostess's salary for my Matterhorn Tours guests, I also earned a generous sum for every excursion. And then there were the tips, the motorbike, and the free, furnished apartment. As Kali said, "Stop fussing with The Prince, dear. You are good for him, he is good for you."

Still, The Prince was searching for a way to organize events where language didn't matter, for tourists from any country. This is where the Greek Night came into play. It was an evening all about eating and dancing, so in The Prince's words, there was "none of that language bullshit." He lined up the perfect venue: the mountain village of Vromorema (literal meaning: "dirty creek", which gives a pretty good impression of the kind of village it was). Vromorema did have a bakery with a brand-new oven inside, and the baker assured The Prince he could handle hot keftedes for up to a hundred diners. The bakery was situated right on the village square, too, where the view to the Turkish coastline was spectacular. On top of that, the local church offered us ten long tables that were normally only used during the village celebrations of the Virgin Mary's feast day on the 15th of August.

So there we were, on that first Greek Night: Two tour buses had transported eighty guests to Vromorema, thereby doubling the village population. The ten long tables were arrayed facing the Turkish panorama, the bouzouki players were warming up their first Theodorakis riffs (Zorba's Dance, inevitably). On top of that, the hostesses had all come along for the night. They had to know what the new event was like that they'd be selling all season, and apart from that, wouldn't it be fun to eat, drink, sing and dance with their colleagues? Even Kali was there, outshining everyone else in her impressive display of jewelry. All seemed to be in place for an unforgettable holiday experience – a fresh breeze, the not-so-distant Turkish coastline shining in the setting sun, and the musicians playing at a volume that made conversation with the person seated next to you just about possible. The only person conspicuously absent was the brain behind the whole operation, The Prince himself.

Lena-with-the-short-fuse emerged angrily from the bakery, headed straight to the table in the back where the season's hostesses had assembled. We'd been hoping for a relaxed, carefree evening to ourselves, just a little apart from the guests who would be happily occupied eating, drinking, dancing, singing and clapping along. The hostess team was a cool lot – we were mostly in our mid- to late-twenties, and we'd often meet after work for a drink or a bite to eat. Kaj and Ragnhild were both from Norway, a Viking poster boy and girl, who'd both get friendlier as they got tipsier. Klaartje from Holland, who was preoccupied with looking for a man because this was her first Greek destination and she didn't like the island one bit – in every way the opposite of the other Dutch hostess, Carina, who had done and seen it all on many a holiday island over her ten years in Greece. Mia from Liverpool was a merry girl whose laugh would dominate any conversation, and who had a penchant for telling great lies while leading tours. Whenever the bus passed an especially scenic beach, she would tell her guests that either Tom Cruise, Tom Selleck, or Tom Jones owned a summer house there. This earned her more tips than anyone else. And then there was Lena-with-the-short-fuse, a tall brunette from Cologne, who was about twice as old as the rest of us. She arrived at our table red in the face and angry as hell. "In all my years in tourism—" she started.

"Oh come on, dear! Don't give us that same old again!" Mia interjected, rolling her eyes. "It's not our fault. Let's just have *fon!*"

Ragnhild, of the Vikings, looked a lot less happy. "I think it's a scandal that The Prince hasn't shown his face..."

Carina and Klaartje rose from the table. Scores of their guests had gathered in the middle of the square. Clearly there was some kind of Dutch revolt in the making, but the girls managed to herd them back to their seats. At the other end of our table, however, the atmosphere seemed to be very different: Our two drivers, Lakis and Yiannis, had brought their wives and kids along, joined by Kali. At their end of the table, it was all laughter and animated Greek – apart from Kali, who had now pulled herself away from the Greek *parea* and was busy managing the situation with some anxiety.

Lena-with-the-short-fuse singled her out, wagging her long index finger at her. Kali got the message. She crossed to the center of the square, and in her smoothest Californian accent, asked all the guests to take their seats. "We are so very, very sorry. You've understood by now that the oven's not working. You will all get your money back. The buses will take you home a little earlier, too, no worries. But as we say on Chios: There's always feta, salad, ouzo, and… Greek dance!"

She snapped her fingers, and the bouzouki players started, right on cue. Meanwhile Viking Kaj and I, the only male hostesses at the table, gave each other a look. "Did you get here on your moped?" he asked me. I nodded – I had a Turkey excursion the next day, which meant waking up at 6 a.m. Kaj gave me a wry smile, "You're smarter than I am. I'll have to wait till everyone's back on the bus and then do the long ride through all the hotels…"

I was about to offer him a ride back when Kali appeared, smiling her Californian smile at Kaj: "Come on handsome, dance with me." But Kaj wasn't interested. "Come on!" she implored. Kaj still wouldn't budge. Then Lena swept in, "Come on, you *Arschloch*! Don't you see what she is trying to do?"

While Kali and Kaj muddled through a partly improvised dance – all spotlights on her impressive jewelry – the baker and his family arrived at the tables bearing eighty portions of Greek salad, along with eighty stone cold cheese pies. Lena tapped me on the shoulder. *"Tanz mit mir,"* she said sternly, and we joined Kali and Kaj on the dance floor. The other hostesses followed suit, and soon we were joined by Yiannis, Lakis, their wives and kids, too. Kali signaled to the musicians and then to us, "Don't stop!" So we didn't. We shuffled along, trying to imitate the skillful moves of Kali, the drivers and their wives, for what felt like eternity but was probably less than half an hour. It must have looked rather desperate – it was. Because around us, eighty disgruntled diners were pushing their cheese pies aside, ignoring their glasses of free ouzo. "Should I invite some of the guests to dance?" I asked Kali. "You will do no such thing!" she shouted back, at deafening volume. "In ten minutes, we'll get the hell out of here!"

In those ten long minutes pretending to do Greek dance moves in a Greek village square, I reflected upon my life as a hostess on Chios so far. I wondered, for instance, why the food served to our drivers and their families smelled so good and even looked positively *warm*? Where on earth had it come from? Another issue was the dancing: My fellow hostesses had come along to experience the Greek Night just this once, but I would be doing this weekly from now on. For them it was a free meal and a curiosity; for me, this was going to be my *work*. In fact, tonight I was getting paid 3,500 drachmae to be here. To dance some traditional Greek dances I didn't know how to. And I never even liked dancing to begin with.

I wouldn't have to worry: The Prince canceled any future Greek Nights before the hostesses even had the chance to launch a common complaint.

2. Guiding with Your Heart

How to describe the beauty of Helena, and what it did to me? It wasn't just those arresting looks and graceful movements, her slender figure and her almond-shaped eyes... she was also the most *immediately physical* woman I had ever known. From the moment I met her, she was touching my arm, rubbing my back, and stroking my hair. There was no holding back with her. In fact, during the whirlwind of our first encounter, I half expected her to throw herself into my arms as soon as an opportunity presented itself. It's easy to chuckle about it now, but back then I was a rather young man with little experience when it came to living the Greek life.

Helena was the island's most experienced tour guide – simply because she lived on Chios, knew an awful lot about the island, and loved sharing that knowledge with anyone she came across. She wasn't exactly a licensed graduate of the Greek Tour Guide School, but she loved her island with a passion. And so, she had become The Prince's standby guide whenever he needed one.

She was in her mid-thirties and lived with a painter who was at least twenty years her senior. He had an impressive, leonine appearance, and not only because of his long gray mane. He owned a quaint stone cottage on a beautiful plot of land, hidden among the endless orchards in the center of the island. From time to time, he would organize an exhibit of his drawings of dilapidated mansions, which were beloved by Chian-Americans (by now I had come to understand there was a sizable community of Chios expatriates and their descendants in New Jersey). It provided him with sufficient income to lead a paradisiacal life among the citrus trees, with the beautiful Helena as his muse. The one child he had, a teenage ne'er-do-well from one of his previous marriages, was temporarily lodged at some boarding school in England.

Whenever a group of foreigners landed on the island, Kali or The Prince would call upon Helena. She'd slip on a long dress, walk down to the main road and wait for the tour bus to pick her up. But when international tourism on Chios began to outgrow its infancy, and more and more Northern European hostesses on mopeds sped by on the streets, The Prince summoned Helena to his office for a serious talk. Only now did he dare to confront her with the many complaints that had accumulated over the years. She was often late. She tired her listeners with drawn-out stories about how Chios was slowly but surely losing its authentic character, telling buses full of foreign travelers that this was due to tourism. The Prince unfurled his list of complaints, Helena raised her pretty eyebrows, cleared her throat, and told him he was talking bullshit. Wasn't she the one who could make even the most insignificant church sound fascinating, captivating her audience with the life story of a local priest? Who except she knew exactly which taverna served the most delicious *kolokythokeftedes*? Who else except she received a stack of Christmas cards each December from happy guests all over the world?

"All true," admitted The Prince, then played the card that would trump all others, "All true. But you don't speak a word of German."

For once, Helena was speechless. So much so she agreed immediately to the next job that The Prince offered her: to introduce the new Dutch guy to the various excursions on offer, to get him up to speed as soon as possible.

For my first excursion, Kali made an itinerary – a checklist of places of interest, listed in chronological order according to the schedule of the tour, with our arrival and departure times scribbled next to them in red. But as soon as Helena got on the bus and introduced herself to me, I understood that we could pretty much throw that checklist out the window. She sat down at the front of the bus and grinned sideways at Lakis, who grumbled something along the lines of, "Here comes trouble again." Helena wore a tight black summer dress and open sandals. Her straw hat obscured most of the view for the thirty-or-so German-speaking guests seated behind her. They looked at each other in confusion – was this their tour guide, some famous Greek actress, or a casual hitchhiker we'd picked up?

Helena then focused her attention on me, making as much body contact as the bumpy bus ride would allow. "Oh, wow, so you're Dutch! What are you doing here? You're cute but so young. Are you even over twenty yet? Haha! Do you have a girlfriend? Hey, your Greek is pretty all right! Anyway, let me tell you what a crazy place this island is..." Whenever I tried to remind her of the presence of the German tourists behind us, she'd turn and address them briefly, explaining the bare minimum about the sights around us in loud, clear American English. Then she turned back to me and resumed our conversation: Yes, she was born in New Jersey, but she'd never go back there again, ever. So, did I live in town? Had The Snake offered me a decent studio? Did Kali try to cozy up to me, as she does with all the new kids? Did I know this tour was just way too standard? Did I want to see more of the island? It has so much else to offer. Just let her know when, and she'd show me around. I did have a motorbike, right?

I was infatuated from the get-go, obviously. But even aside from her being the beautiful Helena, I couldn't have wished for a better person to show me the island. Everywhere we stopped on the excursion that day, she ushered me through a profusion of invaluable details: the best places to stop for photos; the most picturesque streets in the most picturesque villages; the old man who knew where to find the key to a forgotten medieval church; the celebrated Greek writer who lived near a mountain top in a deserted area of the island. He was a famous misanthrope, but if I was interested, Helena could arrange a visit for me...

After an overwhelming morning full of information, new impressions, arm stroking and back rubbing, we arrived at the beach taverna for lunch. One look said it all: dirty tables and chairs, cold *moussaká*, and worn bottles of lukewarm Amstel. Helena and I agreed: this excursion was in need of a revamp. Had I seen that nice restaurant in Olympi? Best cook on the island. "You see? The Snake treats his customers like cash cows. He doesn't care how or where they are fed. He makes the money, while you and I get the complaints. But he is going to have to change his ways a couple of years, when the novelty of Chios has worn off and tourists move on to the next island. Or to Turkey."

After lunch, the group ventured over to a sandy beach nearby – the tour had finished, now it was just a matter of getting them all back on the bus in an hour or two. I found a quiet spot there, too, and observed my guests. There were fifteen couples, who'd each installed themselves about five meters away from the next couple. From a distance, I saw a woman stopping at each of the pairs, making small talk, laughing, rubbing shoulders, and patting heads. It was Helena, of course, looking fabulous in a black bikini. When she caught sight of me, she came over and settled herself only a few inches away. We chatted a bit about this and that, while she sat facing me, cross-legged, playing absent-mindedly with the fingers of my right hand. "Tell me, young man, would you ever have guessed I'm actually approaching forty?" I muttered something like "Of course not," to which she smiled briefly, then leaned forward and stroked my cheek. "I wouldn't have guessed you were twenty-four either. Do you have any sunscreen? That poor back of yours will be red like a lobster's if I don't do anything about it." And with that, she commenced an elaborate back massage that made me relaxed and sleepy...

The next thing I knew, I was being tapped on the shoulder in decidedly un-Helena fashion. I woke up. It was one of the potbellied excursion guests. "*Herr Reiseleiter*? It's time to go!" I scanned the beach around us. Helena waved to me from the water. "Just leave without me!" I'll call you soon!"

Back in the hotel that evening, in a state of total romantic fixation, I read about the women of the island in my brochures about Chios – they had a reputation, apparently, that dated way back, while their men were away at sea for months on end. An Austrian traveler who had visited the island in the seventeenth century couldn't believe his luck. Without a hint of embarrassment, he wrote that if he'd wanted to, he could have hooked up with a different local beauty each night, but there had been no need to resort to that as he chanced upon a very fine *Fraülein* on day two, with whom he eventually married.

This story did little to calm me on that restless night. It would be many years before I realized that Helena's ways were nothing more than the affectionate manner of some Greeks, even to near-strangers in public. Northern Europeans tend to respect each other's private space at all costs, choosing a spot on the bus, at the bar, or at the beach with almost mathematical precision for fear of being seen as intrusive. Greeks, on the other hand, treat these places as one more opportunity to interact with others, as social hubs. To pat one another on the head or even to rub sunscreen on a stranger's back, if necessary. Helena may have been excessive even by Greek standards, but mostly she was just being typically Greek.

In the days and weeks that followed, there would be no private island tour with a goddess on the back of my Yamaha Townmate, wrapping her arms tightly around me. Not because she hadn't meant it when she offered to show me the island. No, it was because of what happened the day after our excursion. When I arrived at the office, Kali took me aside and explained that The Prince wanted me to take over all of Helena's excursions. I tried to protest but Kali reached up and rubbed my left earlobe between her thumb and forefinger – another display of Greekness that I wasn't used to. "Don't you understand, my dear? You're doing really well! You're a born tour guide on the bus, with that friendly smile and all those pretty languages of yours. It will be *so* much easier for The Prince and me, and for all of us, if you just *replace her completely.*"

Kampos Village, Chios, two months later

"Turn left after Taverna Perivoli and keep going, you can't miss it," she'd said. And when the charmingly dilapidated stone cottage loomed before me, I knew she was right. You couldn't miss such an idyllic spot. I parked my motorbike next to the road and took the plastic bag out from where I'd secured it on the back. Inside was a leather jacket from Turkey. The citrus trees around me exuded an intoxicating scent. The cicadas reverberated loudly in the scorching heat. I walked through the tall grass toward the house and tried to catch some of what was going on inside through a side window. It looked dark and deserted. I only heard music. A child's voice singing, accompanied by a melancholy violin and a piano.

A week earlier, Helena had resurfaced. My guests were on the beach, and I had stayed behind in the taverna to drink my fourth *frappé* of the day. Out of nowhere, Helena popped up beside me, just like that. Without saying hello or bothering with other niceties, she asked, "Are you going to Turkey tomorrow?"

An unpleasant feeling shot through me. This was the woman whose job I had taken, and she clearly bore me a grudge. I muttered something about the excursion being the day after that.

"The day after tomorrow? Good. Can you do something for me?"

"Yes, of course." Only too happy to. Anything.

"Here's eighty." She stuffed some dollar bills into my hand. "A few weeks back, I bought a jacket from Hakan in Izmir that needed some repair work. It should be ready by now. He told me it's gonna cost about seventy-five. Can you pick it up for me?"

"Of course. Where do you want me to bring it?"

She explained where she lived and said I could drop by anytime. Then she was gone again, without even so much as a handshake. I sat there as if struck by lightning. Then I counted the dollar bills and stashed them in my trouser pocket.

I tapped against the window and waited. No reply. Finally, I entered through the open front door. The volume of the music increased dramatically when inside, and soon an entire orchestra was booming through the house. I shuffled down the dim hall until I reached the room where the sound originated. In the doorway I stopped for a moment to let my eyes adjust to the darkness. After a few seconds, I noticed a woman lying on a low sofa. Wrapped in a white towel, head also toweled and thrown back, eyes closed. Helena. I coughed, just louder than the surging music. She looked up for a moment, as if moving in slow motion. After a long second, she nodded to me, closing her eyes again. I cautiously approached and placed the leather jacket on the sofa next to her. Then I noticed the portraits in the room. They hung on every wall: Helena, captured by her leonine painter in long, dark strokes. Nude portraits, for the most part. I concentrated my gaze back on the leather jacket.

When the music died, she opened her eyes and took in the jacket. Then she fixed her gaze on me, her almond eyes still half lidded.

"Beautiful music," I managed to say. "Impressive."

"It's Goran Bregovic, from *Time of the Gypsies*. Have you seen that movie?"

"No."

"Then you have to go and see it."

"I haven't been to the cinema in months."

She smiled delicately, "Yeah, you get that way, eh, with all that running around. Thank you for the jacket."

"They rounded it off to $80, so..."

"Yes, I thought they would. You're sweating all over. Do you want something cool to drink, maybe?"

Helena rose from the sofa, not waiting for an answer, and went into the next room, where I heard the tap run. She returned a few minutes later wearing a black dress, the same one that she'd worn on the bus the day we met. She carried a large clay jug of cold water in one hand. Then a new piece of music began, a much faster tune, the orchestra playing like it was the last they'd ever play.

"So, tell me," she said finally.

"Tell you what exactly?" I asked, trying to postpone the inevitable discussion.

Then she touched me unexpectedly. Her index finger ran along my collarbone. She shook her head and smiled a little sadly. "You have lost weight," she said. "They give you a lot to do, don't they?"

"Well, yes… you know how things go with The Pr—"

"So, tell me, now. Has The Snake said anything about me?"

I looked past her, caught that citrus scent again and sighed. "I never really talk to him. But I did talk to the others about it."

"Aha. To Kali, I bet," she said, some contempt in her voice.

"To her and the others."

"Right. And?"

"They said the problem was… I mean, the thing is… that you guide with your heart, not with your head."

"With my heart! Well… that sums it up nicely… "

Helena stood shaking her head, incredulous. She set the jug of water down and sat, staring into nowhere.

After what seemed like hours, she looked up at me, as if only now realizing that I was still in the room with her.

"Thanks again for the jacket," she said at last.

Babis was a short, suntanned man whose age was hard to pinpoint. He wore gold-mirrored sunglasses, plenty of hair gel, and drove an open-roofed SUV, his sound system blaring sultry soul music, which suited the smooth, sweet-talking image he wanted to project. In his own slick way, Babis tried to take advantage of the growing tourist influx. He did a bit of everything: excursions to Turkey, the occasional monastery roundtrip for Greek grandmas, and, last but not least, playing incoming tour operator for SolAir Netherlands, the company for which I'd run the disastrous Mangas tours earlier that year.

As soon as Babis heard that a Dutch *hostess* had joined Chios Travel, he asked The Prince if the new kid would be willing to do something for Babis' SolAir guests. Because the fact of the matter was that he himself hadn't bothered to hire anyone to look after the handful of Dutch that SolAir was going to fly in that season. The Prince considered it for a moment and told Babis, "Fine. Those Dutch oddballs can join our excursions. I already do a Dutch-speaking tour on Monday for the TUI guests. Put them on it. Why not? One thing, though: I'm fine with the new kid selling your guests excursions, but forget about him doing any hostessing for you. No visiting hours, no airport transfers, none of that mollycoddling crap. Just a welcome drink, and that's it. And remember, we share the profit!"

Shortly thereafter, I received a rather syrupy call from Babis: Could I drop by his office? I'd find it just a stone's throw away from The Prince's office, down by the sea front. And indeed, there it was, squeezed in between a bar and a storeroom for fishing nets. His company's name was Epic Travel, its weather-beaten facade not exactly living up to the name. My new friend Babis waited for me in the doorway, his thick graying hair slicked back, a pair of his trademark golden Turkish imitation Ray-Ban sunglasses resting above his remarkably wide nostrils. "Welcome," he murmured in a low voice, accompanied by a weak, clammy handshake. "You want coffee?" His tiny office was barely furnished; there wasn't much besides two tables and two chairs, one for Babis, one for the local Miss Chios, who looked like she had just worked a full shift in a nightclub. Babis smiled as he introduced me to her. "She will do the hostessing for the SolAir people. SolAir people will be happy. Everybody likes a beautiful lady."

"It's very simple, my friend," he continued. Every week, on Thursday, his SolAir travelers would arrive from Holland. "We bring them together, and you sell them excursions. I know SolAir people, they like excursions." Based on my experiences in those Mangas months, that statement was entirely debatable. But Babis persisted, "They are not like TUI or Thomas Cook people." Then he presented me with a financial proposal, before even the *garsoni* from the bar next door could come back carrying a tray with my coffee on it. I would meet the SolAir guests once a week, for about an hour. Miss Chios would collect them from the airport and offer them orange juice. I would just have to be there to present them with the excursion programs run by The Prince, and for any excursion I sold, I would pocket 10 percent. Babis was at pains to explain that it would be the *full* 10 percent – in other words, that this whole excursion-selling business would not be declared to any tax office. There were going to be no excursion tickets, no receipts or checklists.

It didn't take me long to say yes – even though I knew how SolAir operated and saw the similarities in work ethic between self-taught-the-hard-way Mangas and fake-golden-Ray-Bans Babis. What made me decide in favor was plain curiosity about how the operation would work. And even if I earned no more than a few pennies from the whole thing, it would cost me only an hour per week.

From then on, every Thursday afternoon I would meet a group of rather exasperated SolAir guests. Exasperated because at Chios Airport they had been welcomed not by a fresh and smiling hostess but by a shady guy wearing golden sunglasses who, instead of waiting for them attentively, was to be found at the parking lot, chain-smoking with a group of taxi drivers. Then, once he had them all collected, he pushed them into three or four taxis without explanation except, "We come at 4:30 p.m.! Be ready!" Around that hour, Miss Chios would round them up – in, of course, a Nissan Cherry Vanette – and deliver them into the backyard of an anonymous, still unfinished little pension where I would be waiting with three boxes of orange juice, a pile of plastic cups and my excursion pitch. I'd spend the first half hour listening to their complaints: As I was the first fellow Dutchman they met on Chios, this was their chance to share the strange welcome they had just received at the airport. While Miss Chios efficiently served the *jus d'orange* like the professional barwoman that she was, I told my excursion stories, which had an almost magical effect on the guests. Forget those golden sunglasses, forget that flashy barwoman, forget the general feeling of being left in the lurch on the first day of your vacation. Here was a fellow Dutchman extolling the beauty of the island! So let's go see it!

Babis turned out to be right all along: SolAir people did love excursions. In fact, they usually booked two or three excursions per person, which on Chios beat every other foreign tour operator's sign-up rate by miles. At the end of the season, Babis must have raked in enough dough from these excursion-hungry SolAir travelers to comfortably survive the winter. After the last group of the season had left, he again invited me to his office for coffee, where he confessed that he had been a little surprised that I had done my excursion-selling so faithfully, without ever complaining about the money. After all, I'd done the biggest share of the work and only gotten a 10-percent piece of the cake. He walked into his office, came right back and pressed 5,000 drachmae into my hands, a rather stingy tip for more than a dozen weeks spent selling excursions to his guests. He patted me on the back. "Remember, in this business you have to make all your money in the season. You have to be ready for winter."

The thing was, though, Babis didn't know the full story.

Enter Klaartje, the Dutch TUI hostess that season, who led the Monday excursion in Dutch. When The Prince told her that there would be a few extra SolAir people joining, she bluntly replied that it wasn't going to happen. In the contract TUI had signed with The Prince, there was a double exclusivity clause, which stated that the excursions for Dutch TUI guests would be done in Dutch only, and for TUI guests only.

The Prince changed quickly into The Snake. He threatened, he hissed, and he paced around Klaartje's desk, but she wouldn't back down. She told me later that evening that she intended to inform TUI headquarters about this inadmissible little pas de deux between The Prince and Babis. Unless…

Klaartje and I looked at each other – clearly, we had hit upon the same line of thinking. What if we didn't tell Babis and The Prince entirely what was happening? As in: What if I told Babis I had sold ten excursions, while in fact I'd sold fourteen to the SolAir guests? There were no tickets, no receipts, no checklists. All I would have to do was give Babis the amount equivalent to ten excursion tickets, then inform Klaartje there would be fourteen extra guests going on the bus, on top of her TUI guests. If that meant Klaartje and I could share the amount of four excursion tickets, she would be perfectly happy to forget about the double exclusivity clause in the TUI contract.

It worked like a charm – as long as we didn't smuggle more than four extra guests on the bus. To the bus driver, a nearly full bus was a nearly full bus. He wasn't going to do a headcount himself. And as for the guests, the more people on the Double Dutch Bus, the merrier. In any case, none of the SolAir guests were going to want to talk to Babis again after his messy airport welcome. They had no idea who that smarmy guy was in the first place, and Babis was happy to keep it that way.

The arrangement kept everybody happy throughout the season. And by the time the last group of SolAir travelers had gone back home, Babis wasn't the only one ready for the winter.

4. Get on With It, Papadakis!

Mr. Papadakis was a heavy man of advanced age with a drab, chain-smoker's face. On the day I met him, he was wearing a salmon-colored suit and had on a pair of pitch-black sunglasses, Onassis-style. We were at an outdoor restaurant, and he could be seen passing from table to table, shaking people's hands, clasping them amicably by the shoulders and listening to their accounts with a most serious look on his face. From time to time, he could be heard jumping into a conversation, quietly at first but then passionately shifting into top gear, speaking furiously and emphasizing his points with a repertoire of theatrical movements. I was there with my hostess colleagues, and he made a point of skipping our table – probably assuming we were a bunch of tourists, and tourists wouldn't win him any votes in the next election. Because Mr. Athanasios Papadakis was Member of Parliament representative for Chios.

We did have a Greek at our table, Lakis the bus driver, who was seated next to me. Papadakis singled him out in the end – "*Yasou, Laki*! How's the bus, old boy? Things still rolling?" Lakis muttered affirmatively, like a shy schoolboy. Next, Papadakis gave me a sharp and inquisitive look. "Do you understand Greek? Hm. But you are not Greek. A Dutchman? Work here as a tour guide? Hm." And then he was gone, already at the next table, talking about the Cultural Center of Chios that, if all went according to plan, would absolutely, *positively* reopen after the summer. When Papadakis had progressed three tables further, I heard someone complain to him about my colleagues and me. "It is a shame that tourists are shown around by that bunch of

German students over there. As if there are no Greek tour guides! Why don't you get on with it, Papadakis!"

When I recounted this at the office, The Prince and Kali exchanged knowing looks and chuckled. "Ah, that *malákas* Papadakis!" The Prince exclaimed. It was the same tune every year. "If it were up to him, I would be obliged to hire only official guides for the tour bus. And do you know how much that would cost me? Twenty-fucking-thousand drachmae for one morning's work! And as crazy as that sounds, don't think for a minute that I could actually find an official guide here on the island! No, Chios is not good enough for them. They all swarm like flies around the Acropolis, Delphi and Ancient Olympia."

"It's true," Kali added. "Suppose we wanted to hire them, we'd have to pay to fly them over as well."

She pinched my cheek. "Don't you worry. Do you really think there's anything illegal in your grabbing the mic on the bus? You could be singing a song, for all I care, or just counting the passengers. What we don't want you to do is any tour guiding at official archaeological sites. And you know how many we have of those on the island, right?"

"Not a single one!" The Prince grinned. "Just be careful with the monks of Nea Moni. Last month we had fifty Norwegians in the monastery church, and that crazy Ragnhild led them behind the iconostasis. They even walked around the altar, like if it was some fucking *dance*."

"An absolute no-go." Kali said, with the most serious expression.

The Prince patted me on the back. "But you won't get us into trouble, right?"

Within a week of my encounter with Papadakis, the tourist police raided the Chios Travel office, searching for foreign hostesses without work permits. But the birds had already flown the coop. The Prince had been tipped off by one of his cousins on the force. Not that my colleagues and I didn't have work permits, but such a raid created a lot of hassle with forms, paperwork and other time-consuming bother that The Prince couldn't stand. So, when he received a phone call that the police were on their way, he hurriedly sent all of his foreign staff out for coffee – "Order one for me, too: a *mètrio*, no milk."

The policemen were gone before we'd even been served. The Prince came striding out of his office and joined us at the cafeteria with a satisfied smirk on his face. "Bloody politicians," he mumbled. "That Papadakis guy wastes more money in one week than I earn in a whole year. If he had any brains, he would understand that, slowly but surely, tourism is becoming the main source of income here. But when you ask for money for a few good roads? Or a decent runway?" He spread his arms to indicate the port of Chios Town and in a louder voice exclaimed, "All this you see here was built by the bloody Ottomans more than two hundred years ago!"

The Prince shook his head, "Ah, Papadakis... why don't you get on with it."

5. Greco-Turkish Relations

"Ah, thank god you're here, my friend! Tell me *somethienk*: You're going to Izmir, right?"

The fat Greek had stopped right in front of me. He was sweating, he was gesticulating, he was talking loud and rashly – and apparently, he found himself in a difficult spot.

It was Michalis, an endearing and engaging fellow who, with his twenty years in shipping, had seen more of the world than I ever would. Once he passed his fortieth birthday, however, his family had encouraged him to start the next phase of his life. So he had married a local island girl fourteen years his junior, fathered three children, and invested in a souvenir shop. While Michalis was the boss, or as he called it, the "executive manager," his wife did the actual running of the business.

In winter, when tourism on Chios fell silent, Michalis kept himself busy by visiting distant foreign friends and by attending numerous international tourism fairs. During the summer, as it now was, he could be found in the port every day, chatting amiably with anyone who would lend him an ear, doing a little bit of business here and there. Only once did I see him inside his crowded shop, where he was embroiled in titanic battle with a giant inflatable plastic crocodile, gasping for air like a fish out of water.

Michalis' sausage-like fingers rested on my shoulder. Today he was planning to hop over to Turkey and meet his friend Hakan in Izmir. He had bought a ticket from his business acquaintance Babis – the owner of Epic Travel –, but when he got on board he discovered that his ticket was only valid for entry to the Turkish seaside village where the ferry from Chios docked. Fortunately for Michalis, I was doing an Izmir tour that day. "So, I can come with you, right?" he asked. No problem, Michali, my pleasure. There's room enough for everyone on our bus to Izmir, and after more than a dozen of those excursions, I welcomed any kind of diversion.

With the local Turkish guide at the front of the bus painting the rosiest possible picture of his country, Michalis and I were pleasantly in conversation at the back. He was telling me with great enthusiasm about his grand plans. "Take my friend Hakan in *Smyrni*, for example. We are going to set up a huge business together! We'll discuss it today. You must meet Hakan from Hakan Antilop, the leather shop!"

I was happy to inform Michalis that I already knew Hakan, as his leather shop was a highlight of our weekly Izmir trip. Hakan offered the guests apple tea and *loukoum*, decked them out in leather, and always passed me an envelope afterwards. But the ventures that Michalis had in mind were of a different magnitude. Once inside the leather shop, Michalis ran up to

Hakan and threw his arms around him. Hakan seemed rather embarrassed and led Michalis efficiently toward the exit, adding drily, "Let's go for lunch." I left my guests in the able hands of the Turkish guide and tagged along with my two new friends to an exquisite restaurant perfectly suited for hatching plans. There was no kebab but instead delicious homemade kofta, bulgur and pilaf. No Efes beer but a good Italian white wine. No plastic chairs but three Ottoman-style *polythrones*. As Michalis and Hakan raised their glasses to a future collaboration, I was growing more and more curious about it.

"Look here, my friend. Hakan and I are waiting for the tariff walls betweenTurkey and Greece to disappear. As soon as that happens, I will be Hakan's agent in Greece, and he will be mine in Turkey. We are opening a leather shop on Chios, but definitely also one in Athens. Here's to the leather shop in Athens!" Michalis beamed and glistened with sweat. "Hakan, how is your family? Your son wasn't well last time, right?" Hakan, who had discreetly ordered a cola in the meantime, murmured that his son was doing much better. He showed me a picture of a smiling little man in big blue overalls, two crutches under his arms. Michalis searched frantically for a picture of his daughter, too, a doll-like creature all dressed in pink. "Look, what a *koukla*! We've already arranged the wedding! In sixteen or seventeen years, right? Hahaha! Here's to the bridal couple!" My eyes went from one photo to the other. I remarked that they could have been twins. Michalis agreed with a hearty slap on the back, but Hakan kept quiet. His lack of response reminded me of what he had told me a few weeks ago about Greco-Turkish relations: with the current batch of corrupt politicians in charge, nothing would ever change.

Michalis, however, was of a more optimistic disposition. A week later, he was waiting for me at the Chios customs check early in the morning. He handed me a white plastic bag of bloody pork chops, certainly about five pounds or so. "My friend! Going to Izmir, eh? I know Hakan loves these, but he can't buy them anywhere over there. Could you do me a very, very big favor?"

It was a Sunday afternoon like any other and I had just gotten back from the usual boat excursion stopping at several beaches around the island. The guests had disembarked sunburned and tired but content. While I stood chatting with the crew – Yes, it had been a choppy sea but no one had been sick, thank god – I spotted some guys on the quay headed our way. It was Yiannis and Sakis, two crew members of the *Diamantaki,* a small excursion boat The Prince used for day trips now and then, and they looked worried. My friend Kostas was with them, and he, too, had an unusually serious expression. The question they asked when they reached us sounded very ominous. "Did anything happen today?"

"No, nothing. Why?"

Yiannis, Sakis and Kostas breathed a sigh of relief.

"What happened to you then?" I asked anxiously.

Kostas told me to sit down first, and began to explain. While he was out at sea testing out the new engine on his boat, he received panicky messages from Yiannis and Sakis onboard the *Diamantaki*. Kostas quickly set course for it. As he came alongside, he saw a group of men onboard, all of them seismologists who had gone out to do research at the nearby volcanic beach that morning. They stood huddled together in fear on the lower deck. Yiannis and Sakis stood alone at the back of the boat, pointing at something trailing in the wake of the *Diamantaki*. When Kostas got closer, he saw that they were two human bodies.

"Who are they?" Kostas called out, to which Yiannis and Sakis could only shake their heads. Kostas immediately alerted the port police, who ordered him to pull the bodies onto his boat as quickly as possible. Sakis took the seismologists back to the harbor, while Yiannis stayed behind on Kostas' boat. It took a great effort, but together they managed to lug the two swollen bodies out of the water. "My god, they were heavy, and big like whales!" Kostas said, his eyes wide.

They had found travel documents on one of the bodies – Kurdish names, Turkish passports. When the port police arrived, they requested Kostas join in the macabre search for other bodies. Eventually, a fleet of local fishermen joined as well. Together, they pulled fifteen other bodies out of the water that afternoon. Only one survivor was found, who was saved thanks to a large piece of driftwood. This man told the port police that he had been on a small raft with thirty other Kurds. It was the kind of boat that regularly departed from Turkey for the Greek islands under the cover of night, arranged by smugglers who charged each passenger hundreds of dollars to make the crossing, even though Chios lies just a few miles off the Turkish coast. The Turkish coast guard usually turned a blind eye – the authorities didn't mind offloading a few more troublesome Kurds. Once in Greece, the Kurds would be granted political asylum and then, most often, move on to relatives elsewhere in the world.

This particular raft had made the crossing on a Saturday night in the middle of summer, when the northern *meltemi* wind was roaring at forty knots. It had been too much for the raft, and the passengers had been unable to save themselves on the stormy sea. Over the course of the day, as my tourist-packed pleasure boat chugged peacefully along the picturesque harbors of northeastern Chios, the bodies of the drowned were being fished out of the water off the southeastern coast.

By the end of the day, the police search had recovered thirty bodies in total, which matched the statement of the lone survivor. The international press would end up devoting only a few lines to it, even though tragedies like this weren't as common in the early nineties as they would be twenty-five years later. As for The Prince and his colleagues, they went to sleep that night without worrying too much about it. None of the dead bodies had come close to their excursion boats or, for that matter, to the crowded and popular Golden Sand Beach.

Indeed, nothing had happened today.

7. Sex and Games

"Make sure you play games with them."

"Games?" I asked innocently. "What kind of games?"

The Prince eyed me sternly. "Well, you know, cards, Scrabble, chess… Keep them busy, or they'll start grumbling."

It was late September and the autumn brought in cooler weather, which meant that soon the first British SAGA group of the season would arrive on Chios. SAGA was an international tour company specializing in travel for the elderly, and the elderly preferred to travel when the scorching heat of the Greek summer had abated. Kali had bestowed on me a pile of SAGA brochures, by way of saying that I'd be the hostess du jour for this group of vacationers. While leafing through the material, I marveled at what I saw. There was not one single photo of well-fed families in garish swimsuits, frolicking in L-shaped pools. No, the SAGA approach was much more subtle. They advertised their vacation packages with thoughtfully written presentations of the historical and cultural context of each destination. These were accompanied by photos of archaeological ruins and other cultural landmarks, printed on glossy, high-quality paper. Only occasionally were the texts interrupted by hotel photos showing classy lounges such as the one at the Chandris Hotel – the one where I'd imagined Sean Connery as an early James Bond, and where the SAGA guests would spend their entire stay on the island.

None of us knew what SAGA really stood for, but that didn't stop my colleagues and me from having a go at this mysterious acronym. First prize went to Lena, the German TUI hostess with the short fuse and more than twenty-five years of tourism experience, who came up with "Send a Granny Away". From what she had heard and seen, she said, SAGA guests were sweethearts, as long as you gave them plenty of attention without pampering them too obviously. Still, would these British old-timers really be expecting to play *games* every evening?

According to The Prince, this kind of entertainment was a regular part of the SAGA package. I just nodded and thought to myself, "No way." So, the first night I apologized for the fact that there were no games available this season. I saw eyebrows rise. Oh no, this could mean trouble.

"No games? What kind of games were you thinking of?" one of the ladies asked, with some of that all-too-British sarcasm. I was at a loss for an answer, and the whole party erupted into laughter. "Don't worry," she said, looking at my puzzled face. "We'll be perfectly fine without Scrabble and such."

At the end of that first day, the Wilkinson couple approached me a little awkwardly. They hoped I didn't mind, and they were awfully sorry to disturb me with this issue of theirs… But could I please come along to their hotel room? There was quite a problem, they were afraid to admit. I entered their room prepared for a flooded bathroom or an exploded TV set. Instead, Mr. Wilkinson indicated an innocent Rowenta kettle they had brought, with a British electrical plug. The problem was, you see, that the plug didn't fit into the Greek socket. And yes, the Wilkinsons did own an adapter, but they had forgotten it at home – *silly us*! And again, they would completely understand if it simply wasn't possible, but could such an adapter perhaps be acquired? That is to say, were they sold in this part of the world?

It was no problem at all. An adapter for "small personal electronics" could be easily bought in town. After all, as I was keen to inform them, Chios had entered the twentieth century a good while ago.

A more immediate problem arose in connection with eighty-three-year-old Reverend Burns. His wife informed me matter-of-factly that her dear husband had forgotten to pack the medication for his "heart ailment". She hoped the Chios pharmacies would be able to help, otherwise there might be "a bit of an issue" in the days to come. It was a good thing, then, that Greek pharmacies have always been among the most well stocked in the world.

As soon as the small personal electronic device had been successfully connected to the Greek power grid and the heart medication was secured from a nearby pharmacy, the group of elderly Britons became absolutely enchanted by the island of Chios. They joined on every excursion and asked hundreds of questions about everything. They all ordered the local specialty of roasted mutton giblets and feasted on it, about which the dumbfounded waiter remarked, "They eat it! Are you sure they come from *Anglía*?" They took boat trips, climbed narrow paths up to various viewpoints, and Reverend Burns, all pepped up with some small help from the pharmacy, routinely ventured into the warm September sea at Agia Pelagia Bay. On the group's last night, they invited me to a celebratory dinner, where I confessed that they had been by far the nicest group of the season. We raised quite a few glasses to everyone's health, until John, the joker of the group, said to me, "And now off you go, my boy! It's time for those games."

"Games?" I asked, a little baffled.

"You do know what SAGA stands for, don't you?"

I realized I was finally going to hear it. Then John answered, with a big grin on his face: "Sex and Games for the Aged."

The next day, all that was left was the transfer to the airport, where my new SAGA friends would board their flight back to the UK. When we arrived at the check-in counter, I explained that they could collect their boarding passes here by presenting their plane tickets. Eleven paper tickets emerged from as many travel bags – all except Mrs. Johnston's. She just stood there, petrified and blushing all over.

"Oh my goodness," she finally uttered. "Was that ticket also necessary for the return journey?"

Mrs. Johnston, thinking that she would be getting a second ticket on Chios, had thrown hers away – not a clever thing to do in the times before electronic flight records and online check-ins. But wait – Mr. Johnston thought he remembered seeing the ticket in the trash can! Yes, now Mrs. Johnston remembered, too. When she had emptied her purse in the hotel room, she had tossed the ticket into that red pedal bin next to the toilet.

In the airport parking lot, Lakis was just preparing to drive his bus back to town. I hopped on board and told him to drive to the Chandris as fast as he could. Room 113, and let's hope the cleaning ladies haven't done their job too thoroughly the past few days.

Don't throw paper in the toilet! is the most familiar text spotted in any tourist bathroom in Greece, whether in a hotel, restaurant or cafe. The pipes used in Greek plumbing systems are usually so narrow that they can clog up in no time with lavish use of toilet paper – and one walk through any Greek supermarket will tell you that Greeks, indeed, consume large quantities of it. *Throw wastepaper in basket please!* is the standard advice. At the four-star Chandris Hotel, every bathroom had a shiny red pedal bin by way of basket. As I pressed my foot on the pedal, I said a quick prayer.

I carefully lifted the plastic bag out of the bin, holding it by its very edges, and spun it around. There, at the very bottom of that used paper mass, I saw the Heathrow–Chios–Heathrow paper ticket. I tipped the contents of the plastic bag back into the bin, until I was able to fish the ticket out. I wrapped it in a long piece of fresh toilet paper, washed my hands thoroughly and left the hotel room. In the hallway, I bumped into the cleaning ladies just about to enter room 113.

On my rush back to the airport, the taxi driver asked what that smell was, and if I had become a new father. I told him the story. "You must write this down!" he cried, laughing. "It's too funny!" Indeed, I thought, it would make a great story. Then again, when I discreetly handed Mrs. Johnston her ticket, one look at her red face was enough to suggest that if I wrote the story, I'd better wait a good while before trying to publish it.

8. Reading Coffee

By the time October rolled around, Chios had returned to its normal rhythms. Students were attending their first lectures at the local naval college, the cultural center was organizing symposia on the historical importance of Homer's *Odyssey*, the cinema and theater had reopened, and as for the beach hotels, one after the other closed their doors for the winter. Yes, the tourist season was over, and Chios had transformed again into the hustling and bustling island it had always been, as its inhabitants have long had a knack for shipping and business. Like a migratory bird, I understood that these developments would soon lead me to my own departure.

In those last weeks, with more spare time on my hands than before, I chugged around on my good old Yamaha Townmate. Early autumn found Chios at its mildest, even the meltemi winds had moved elsewhere, and everything seemed to radiate a warm and pleasant glow. I visited the local theater, which was presenting a production of an ancient tragedy by Euripides, with the ominous title *The Beautiful Helena*. I found a copy of the play at the local library to look over before the performance. To me, the story read like a far-fetched affair: the joyful reunion of two lovers long separated by war and fate, with a happy ending owed to one of the silliest plot-twists ever devised when Helena's twin brothers, Castor and Pollux, improbably drop in from the afterlife to help her out. Through all this, the legendary significance of Helena as the woman whose beauty and vanity "toppled Troy and ruined Greece" is put into question. According to Euripides, Helena wasn't even at Troy, which makes her husband, Menelaos, realize that "we fought for a shadow and died for a shadow."

Still, I bought a ticket – of course I did. I had an inkling who would play the lead role as the beautiful Helena, and I wasn't disappointed. There she was, in one of her characteristic black dresses, dominating the stage, reducing any actor who dared approach her to mere rubble. Helena herself – freelance tour guide, part-time actress, perfectly capable of toppling Troy and ruining Greece any old day – playing Helen of Troy the same way she used to lead her tours: with her heart.

Before the hostesses took flight to their winter destinations, The Prince ordered a round of coffee and announced he had a little present for us all. It had been a good season, he said. We had done our best. So, he wanted to treat us to an excursion to Turkey, including a night at the lavish, thirty-three-story Izmir Hilton. A wild cheer broke out. My colleagues were clearly taken by surprise after all our strained dealings with The Prince. But I kept quiet and exchanged glances with Kali. She had already told me of The Prince's little present the previous evening, warning me that I wouldn't be part of the deal. On the day of the Hilton trip, I'd have a last excursion to run for representatives from Austria's main outgoing tour operators. It was crucial they got to see Chios at its best: If the excursion was a success, it would increase The Prince's chances of winning numerous profitable contracts with Austria next year. "And as you can guess," Kali said, a little sadly, "I'm not going to Izmir either. Someone's got to hold down the fort."

Did I protest? Did I raise hell? I'd been to Izmir dozens of times that season, and frankly, the concrete jungle of Athens seemed like a jewel compared to Turkey's decidedly unattractive third-largest city. I didn't care much for Hiltons with king-size beds and swimming pools at an altitude of 150 meters either. Still, I couldn't just quietly accept the fact that The Prince would be so generous to his foreign crew, and let his own staff down.

"Just let me handle it," Kali said.

The excursion with the Austrian tour operators turned out to be a disaster on every level. For starters, they had brought along an archaeologist whose main ambition seemed to be interrupting my guiding of the tour. So, there we were, he and I, each fighting for the microphone. It got to the point where, during my usual introduction of the village where we were about to have lunch, the eager archaeologist started shouting in English, "You must mention the church bells! The church bells! *Das Glockenspiel!*"

During lunch, I called Kali from the taverna, ready to threaten her with my immediate resignation. No one in the office answered the phone. Dammit. She had probably gone off to the beach and left me with these obnoxious Austrians! But when I left the taverna, there she was in front of me, wearing her lovely ochre-colored dress and her distinctive Kali grin.

"So. Your tour for the day is over. Where would you like to go?"

"You left the office unattended?" I asked.

She stroked my cheek and kept grinning, "Well, the boss won't be back till tomorrow."

I stroked her cheek back, "Take me to the Blue Lagoon, then."

So we walked off, hand in hand, watched by forty stupefied Austrians and a driver who couldn't stop laughing.

"Look. I have 200 dollars here. Our hush money for the day. Be grateful, be very grateful for the hold I have on The Prince. Let's go spend it. Someplace where nobody knows me. I happen to know something nearby."

Kali drove me to Sidirounda, up north. Sidirounda wasn't even a village, just a handful of scattered summer houses that were already boarded up for winter, near yet another deserted beach. What Sidirounda did have was a taverna called The Aegean Panorama. And indeed, the view from the outdoor terrace was nothing short of majestic. The mighty blue Aegean Sea surrounded us. Far in the hazy distance, you could make out the contours of other islands. The terrace was totally empty, and a deep silence reigned supreme.

Kali and I chose the table nearest to all that Aegean blue and sat down. A waiter came out – not the usual taverna guy but a young man dressed to a tee. With his hair combed back, expensive shirt, stylish glasses and solemn expression, he looked entirely out of place. As I studied the menu, the waiter's appearance started to make more sense. At The Aegean Panorama, you could easily spend 200 dollars in one afternoon. That was exactly what we set out to do, starting with a couple of white wines from the most exclusive Pelopponnesian wineries.

"This is the only place on Chios where they don't know you?" I asked Kali.

"Yes. This is where I always take my lovers."

We devolved into laughter. Meanwhile, something seemed to be wrong with the waiter. He kept his distance but cast weird looks in my direction.

"Do I know this guy?" I whispered to Kali.

"Impossible. He hates Chios. He's just here because his parents run this place in summer, and he needs the cash."

"Don't we all."

"Wait, I'll make him go away."

She slid over to me and sat herself on my knee. We started exchanging kisses. Soon the waiter disappeared.

"This sure beats the Izmir Hilton, no?"

More laughter, more wine. Our life stories, in bits and pieces. Kali would be leaving Chios soon as well. She had a job lined up in Athens, a serious job. Management.

"So how about you, Mister Hostess? How's your experience in tourism been so far?"

I answered that so far, I couldn't complain.

Kali got up and looked out at the setting sun. "Seriously now."

"In all honesty, I haven't got the faintest idea what I'll be doing a month from now."

More laughter, more wine.

When at length we asked for the bill, the waiter shot me a look I just couldn't ignore.

"Is something wrong?" I asked him.

He sighed, and answered in Greek, "You really don't recognize me then, do you?"

Wait a second. Now that I heard that voice. But the man? Not yet thirty, with those glasses…

"Sorry, but I can't place you."

"Well, I can sure place *you*. You stood in the middle of the road, stranded without gasoline, when I was passing that way for a delivery. All alone in the middle of nowhere. About four months ago."

Young Woody Allen! The driver of the yellow truck! The young graduate who had saved me on day one, and whom I'd told then I was here on vacation. I felt a blush rise to my face. He saw it and laughed, much friendlier now. "I had a hunch already back then that you weren't just another tourist."

I explained the story to Kali, who uttered a string of *Oh my gods*! Young Woody gave her a wry smile, "He never even told you?"

"We almost fired him on day one over this!" she said to him. "You saved his sorry Dutch ass!"

Young Woody chuckled and said, "Coffee's on the house."

By the time we got to the car, the sun had set and October was sending chilly gusts of wind down my spine. On the way back, Kali asked, "So, what about the rest of your life?"

I had kept my private affairs off limits to my colleagues for most of the season. In the end, Vasso had come to Chios for a long stay in summer. And now she was pressuring me to come back to Athens as soon as I could.

I shrugged and said, "Someone is waiting for me back home."

"Hmm. Tell me about it. My fiancé is in Athens, too."

"Really?"

"Yup. There is a good chance I'll be married next year."

That sobered me up a good deal. "We've been wise today, haven't we?"

"Yep. Wise and boring."

As I waited in line to go through security, I saw my two suitcases being hauled into the belly of an Olympic Airways aircraft bound for Athens. I had left the motorbike at the empty office and said a quick goodbye to The Prince. He had been on the phone shouting at someone on the other end, and had merely dismissed me with an *off you go* gesture.

As the plane took off, I surveyed the island from above, recognizing every bend in the road below me. I wondered what the next few months would bring. And I reflected on my last minutes with Kali, at the airport cafe. She had offered to read my coffee.

"Read my *what*?" I asked, baffled once more.

She picked up my cup of Greek coffee, which by now contained only the soggy remains of coffee grinds, placed the saucer over the top and turned everything upside down in one quick motion. She left the coffee cup upended on its saucer for about five minutes. Finally, she picked it up, turned it back over and peered inside. After what seemed like forever, she spoke, almost intoxicatingly slow: "I see five roads. Five roads that are open to you. And you are at that five-way junction. But..." and here she let her voice grow louder, "you don't know which way to go!" She sighed. "It is time you made a choice because it all looks very confusing! You have to stand for something in your life. Do not postpone everything all the time. Do not procrastinate!"

I produced a painful grimace, struck by the sudden realization that Kali was right. Perhaps it was about time to realize that I had a university diploma, that my friends in the Netherlands were all busy with careers and their first mortgages, and that someone was there waiting for me in Athens.

Kali tried to put me at ease. "Your future is wide open," she said, "but we already knew that, didn't we?"

I looked into her eyes. "Am I going to see you again?"

She grinned her grin and said, "Maybe."

Then I reached for Kali's coffee cup. "My turn now to read your future."

Her hand seized my wrist again. "You will do no such thing!"

The plane quickly left Chios behind and would soon be landing in Athens. The flight was not even an hour long, but to me it felt like a journey from one universe to another.

I closed my eyes. Kali's coffee-reading had moved me more than I dared admit. It didn't matter that what she showed me was the spent coffee grounds in my cup running down in five streaks, or that she had dreamed up some story in explanation. I didn't see sludge there; I truly saw the five roads, each more winding than the next. Which one was I supposed to take?

About six months later, I became a hostess on the island of Lesvos.

About the Author

Ruard Wallis de Vries (1967) has worked and lived in Greece on and off since the early 1990s. The short stories in this book cover his first forays into the Greek everyday. Apart from regular contributions to travel magazines, Ruard has also published in the Dutch national press on the Greek economic crisis and on the refugee situation on the Greek islands. Since 2012, he has been organizing film festivals where Greek short films and documentaries take central stage. Last but not least, he bought and renovated a handful of charmingly dilapidated island houses on Samos and Leros – a book about his experiences as a house owner on the Greek islands is currently in preparation.

Some of the stories in this book were originally published in Dutch newspapers and magazines back in the 1990s. At the outbreak of the COVID-19 pandemic, Ruard revisited these stories, recruiting a few critical Anglophone friends in order to prepare this translation into English. Although the action takes place in the last decade of the twentieth century, it is perhaps telling that very few updates to the text were necessary.

Still, any resemblance of this book's characters with existing persons is, of course, pure coincidence.

The author would like to thank the following persons, without whom this book would never have seen the light of day:

Bente Kristin Bruu – who did the wonderful illustrations and who offered plenty of sound suggestions

Konstantinos Frangoulis – film director, music buddy and photographer with Greek island roots, who shot the photo on the back cover

Andy Gibbs – "critical friend," fellow philhellene and classic rock aficionado, who was the first to proofread these stories

Freek Huson – longtime friend and editor, who offered the sudden opportunity to publish

Angelica Sgouros – copyeditor, who did a brilliant job fishing out hundreds of *Hollandisms* – and much more

Lisa Stang – astute proofreader, who actually knows what a *Sieb* means